TRUE OR FALSE

DETERMINING WHAT WE BELIEVE AND WHY WE BELIEVE IT

LEADERS GUIDE

Josh McDowell

Visit Tyndale's exciting Web site at www.tyndale.com

True or False Leaders Guide

Edited by Lynn Vanderzalm

Printed in the United States of America

ISBN 0-8423-8014-0

1. Undated Elective Curriculum/Primary (Grades 1 and 2)
2. Undated Elective Curriculum/Middler (Grades 3 and 4).
3. Undated Elective Curriculum/Preteen (Grades 5 and 6).

TRUE OR FALSE

TABLE OF CONTENTS

ABOUT THE AUTHOR

The content of the *True or False Workbooks* is based on Josh McDowell's Beyond Belief to Convictions book and the messages to youth he has developed.

Josh is an internationally known speaker, author, and traveling representative of Campus Crusade for Christ. He has authored or co-authored more than sixty books, including *More Than a Carpenter* and *The New Evidence That Demands a Verdict*. Josh and his wife, Dottie, have four children and live in Texas.

ABOUT THE WRITERS

Kevin Johnson and Cindy Pitts collaborated with the Josh McDowell team to create the overall scope and direction of the *True or False Workbook* course based on Josh McDowell's writings and messages. Kevin completed the first draft. Cindy modified, reworked, and field-tested the material.

Cindy Pitts is Minister of Children at Houston's First Baptist Church. She brings over twenty years of full-time experience with children to her writing abilities. Cindy has authored or co-authored numerous children's curriculum including Josh McDowell's *Truth Works, KidShare: What Do I Do Now?* and *Good News for Kids: The Power to Change Lives*. Cindy and her husband, Ron, have one child and live in Texas.

Kevin Johnson is a writer and speaker. He has written and co-authored over twenty books to youth, including *Can I Be a Christian without Being Weird, Catch the Wave*, and *Children Demand a Verdict* with Josh McDowell. Kevin and his wife, Lyn, have three children and live in Minnesota.

Acknowledgments

We would like to thank the many people who brought creativity and insight to forming this Leaders Guide:

The children's ministry team in Houston that field-tested this material.

Lynn Vanderzalm of Tyndale House Publishers for her guidance and wise counsel on the content and for helping us communicate each concept clearly.

Dave Bellis, my (Josh's) resource development coordinator for twenty-six years, for helping us focus the message of this workbook and managing the maze of details to bring this work to completion.

Patty Crowley for her skillful and timely editing, and Bob Hostetler for his editorial oversight.

Jim Baird, who, as the production manager, kept the process rolling and worked through the maze of details to bring the work to the typesetting stage.

And finally, to the campaign team at Tyndale House, who so graciously endured the process with us.

Josh McDowell

True or False

INTRODUCTION
by
Josh McDowell

THE NEED FOR A SPIRITUAL REVOLUTION

Research reveals that our children and young people are in a precarious position. Though many of the children involved in church and in Christian families make a profession of faith in Jesus Christ in their formative years, that decision alone does not equip them to face the spiritual challenges of their generation.

As incredible as it may seem, research shows that "accepting Christ" and making a profession of faith today make little to no difference in a young person's attitude and behavior. You have probably seen the statistics. Seventy-four percent (74%) of our Christian teenagers say they cheat on school tests; eighty-three percent (83%) say they lie to their teachers; ninety-three percent (93%) lie to their parents; and sixty-three percent (63%) say they become physically violent toward others when angered.[1] These actions represent no more than a four-percentage point difference from the behaviors of those who profess no Christianity at all!

Sixty-four percent (64%) of our young people believe that "if a person is generally good or does enough good things for others during their life, they will earn a place in heaven."[2]

To our kids, Christ's teaching of love and doing good is what Christianity is all about. As a children's worker, you have the opportunity to help keep those you minister to from embracing these distorted beliefs and wrong behavior. If something is not done now, your children will probably accept the beliefs of current church teenagers. Here is what our present teenagers believe:

- 63 percent don't believe Jesus is the Son of the one true God;
- 58 percent believe all faiths teach equally valued truths;
- 51 percent don't believe Jesus rose from the dead;
- 65 percent don't believe Satan is a real entity;
- 68 percent don't believe the Holy Spirit is a real entity.
- 70 percent don't believe an absolute moral truth exists.[3]

And does any of this matter? We may prefer for our children and young people to embrace biblical beliefs, but what harm will come if they don't? Research consistently

[1] "The Ethics of American Youth—2002 Report Card" conducted and published by Josephson Institute of Ethics (Marina del Rey, Calif.: Josephson Institute of Ethics, 2002).
[2] Barna Research Group, "Third Millennium Teens" (Ventura, Calif.: The Barna Research Group, Ltd, 1999). 49.
[3] Ibid, 51.

shows that what a person believes translates into attitudes and behavior. The vast majority of our young people have distorted beliefs about Christ and Christianity. Those with such distorted views are

- 200 percent more likely to be disappointed in life;
- 200 percent more likely to physically hurt someone;
- 210 percent more likely to lack purpose;
- 300 percent more likely to use illegal drugs;
- 600 percent more likely to attempt suicide.[4]

Something must be done—something different from what we are presently doing to reverse this trend. We need a complete turnaround from where things are with our kids. We need a revolution—a CrossCulture revolution.

What Is a CrossCulture Revolution?

A cultural mind-set has infiltrated our homes and churches and is stealing our kids away from us and robbing them of what true Christianity is—a transformed relationship with God through Christ. It is time for a spiritual revolution—"a fundamental change in the way of thinking; a complete turnaround from the culture." It is time to create a culture of the Cross—a new generation of young people starting in their early years, who know what it means to be a Christian and live accordingly. That is what this course is all about—inciting a spiritual revolution, a CrossCulture revolution.

What is a CrossCulture revolution? It is a fundamental change in the way Christianity is presented to our children and young people. It is a shift from simply leading our kids to accept Christ to leading them to form an intimate relationship with him and embrace deepened convictions about him. It is an effort to create a culture of the Cross—raising up a generation of transformed followers of Christ who know why they believe what they believe.

This *True or False Workbook* is part of a family of product to help you create such a CrossCulture among your young people. This Leaders Guide, along with the *True or False Workbook* for each of your students, is designed to lead younger children (grades 1–3) and older children (grades 4–6) in your church, school, family, or camp to a personal encounter with a loving God.

Keep in mind, however, that the *True or False* course is only a beginning. Raising up a generation of the Cross will require a long-term commitment and process that must continue beyond childhood, into their teen years and beyond. It will take consistent teaching, modeling, and mentoring of your young people in such a culture of the Cross. It will also require working in harmony with the parents of your students and involving the

4. "The Churched Youth Survey," (Dallas: Josh McDowell Ministry, 1994), pp. 65, 69.

leadership within your church to cooperate with you in this effort. And it will require numerous equipping tools that can help you strategically plan and execute your own CrossCulture revolution.

THE EQUIPPING TOOLS FOR YOUR REVOLUTION

We are committed to serving you over the long term. In the past, our various campaigns and events have come to your cities . . . and left. However, if we are to truly see a long-term change take place in the lives of our young people, we need to make a long-term commitment to your ministry on the local level. We are prepared to make such a commitment and provide you with four critical components to incite your own spiritual revolution within your church and group. Because we are serving you and these components are for you, we want you to own them for yourself.

1. My Resources

This *True or False* Leaders Guide and the two *True or False Workbooks* are part of a family of product.

Each child needs a workbook for your group sessions. These workbooks will give them a heightened sense of participation in the content of each session, and a greater sense of ownership of the material being shared. The workbooks encourage thought and interaction, even for the younger children.

Children Demand a Verdict is an excellent complement to the *True or False* sessions and workbooks. It gives children the ability to learn further on their own, and even to explore topics not covered in the *True or False* sessions.

Other resources for individual adults and adult small groups are available. A **Belief Matters** Video Series and Workbook for adults and **The Revolt** Video Series and workbook for teens enable your church to launch a coordinated CrossCulture Revolution to every age group. **Family Devotions, Josh McDowell's Youth Devotions 2,** and supplemental books for adults and youth provide ongoing support in an effort to raise up a generation of passionate followers of Christ who know why they believe what they believe. (More information on this foundational family of products to launch your church-wide and familywide campaign is found on page 25. These products can be ordered by calling toll-free at 888-566-9949 (KNOW WHY), or you can order online at **www.MyCrossCulture.com** and go to the Resource section).

If you haven't already done so, meet with your pastor or church staff to discuss plans for a churchwide emphasis using these foundational resources. The parents of your students are critical in the spiritual and emotional development of your youth group. The ideal scenario is to coordinate

the launch of adult, youth, and children's groups simultaneously. But even if that cannot be arranged, it will be important to eventually get parents and your children's groups utilizing these vital resources.

And this is only the beginning. *True or False* is part of the CrossCulture family of product that focuses on the first characteristic of the CrossCulture life–the transformed life. In the fall of 2004, we will release a new family of product focused on further deepening your students' convictions in the reliability of God's Word and teaching them how to live a life pleasing to God through the power of God's Spirit.

Each year we will continue to release to you relevant resources on the CrossCulture life. Our goal is to provide you with four years of resources that will enable you to adequately raise up a generation of young people who know why they believe what they believe and who are willing and able to live out their biblical convictions regardless of the consequences.

2. My Training

The many resources we have developed over the years for adults, youth, and children's small groups have been regarded as self–led and easy–to–use. However, none of these resources has ever addressed how to build an effective small group within your church–especially a youth group. Yet training in how to create and maintain a thriving youth ministry has been a critical need, and many have requested it. Therefore, we will be collabo-rating together with the most effective youth ministries and youth–group specialists from around the world to bring you the best in youth ministry training.

To start, we will conduct an annual three–day intensive training confer-ence beginning in the fall of 2003. (For more details on this training, visit **www.MyCrossCulture.com** and go to the Training section.) Additionally, we plan to develop a Certified Trainer Program that will establish regional trainers in your area to provide ongoing training. Our goal is to equip you with a revolutionary approach to youth ministry that is grounded in bib-lically relevant messages and methods that generate and perpetuate sacri-ficial and passionate followers of Christ.

3. My Events

Events in and of themselves are not enough to launch and sustain a CrossCulture Revolution. But events do play a critical role in this revolu-tion in inspiring, motivating, and challenging youth and adults to embrace and live out the CrossCulture life.

During each fall and spring, we will be traveling to some thirty cities to conduct three events in each area: a church leader's meeting, adult/parent seminar, and youth event. The focused message of this annual tour will coincide with the message of the product released that year. Encouraging your church leadership, adults/parents, and youth to attend these events will enable you to focus their attention on each foundational message of the CrossCulture life. You can then capitalize on the impact of those events by following up with the complementary CrossCulture resources for your own small group, to help participants apply the event message in their everyday lives. (For more details on the events visit **www.MyCrossCulture.com** and go to the Events section.)

4. My Ongoing E-Connection

Imagine having the wisest and most effective person in ministry today as your constant advisor and mentor. Imagine this person attentively listening to your progress and successes, as well as your struggles and challenges. Then imagine this person offering just the right advice, just the right equipping resources, and just the right event that would effectively address your specific challenge.

With that kind of specialized support, your ministry would probably thrive beyond your imagination. That is precisely our prayer for you, so that kind of mentoring relationship is what we plan to make available to you. We are offering an e-connection that listens to your concerns and struggles, victories and successes. We will pass on your success stories to others. And the struggles and challenges you face will receive special attention.

We will employ the best hearts and minds in ministry to grapple with your needs and come up with tried and proven answers you can apply. Those answers will be developed into training modules or be translated into an equipping resource. Our constant prayer and goal is to always be here as an equipping arm for your ministry. We see our ministry as serving your ministry. That is why we are partnering with others in an umbrella e-ministry called MyCrossCulture.com.

So, to begin our ongoing connection with each other, register at **www.MyCrossCulture.com.** If you have already registered at BeyondBelief.com you are pre-registered at MyCrossCulture.com. The Beyond Belief site and the CrossCulture site have now been combined. The goal of this serving ministry is to provide the necessary networking between the many specialists in youth, adult, and children's ministry and then offer you everything you need to create a generation of sacrificial and passionate followers of Christ. None of us needs to minister alone. We all need each

other. And **MyCrossCulture.com** is your e-connection to receive the best in guidance, help, and support . . . and your means to share with others.

We are in this battle together. But remember, the battle is the Lord's. As you and each of us remain faithful, we will be amazed at what God will accomplish through our respective ministries. We are spiritually connected together in Christ's body. But as we also get connected with each other in other ways, much can be done to honor and glorify God in your own ministry–more than you imagine. As the apostle Paul wrote, "Now glory be to God! By his mighty power at work within us, he is able to accomplish infinitely more than we would ever dare to ask or hope. May he be given glory in the church and in Christ Jesus forever and ever through endless ages. Amen" (Ephesians 3:20–21).

Let the revolution begin!

A FINAL CHECKLIST

As you prepare to launch the *True or False* course, here is a final checklist of reminders.

- ❑ Obtain sufficient quantity of workbooks and other products.
  Each student in your group will need a workbook. You can obtain more workbooks at your Christian supplier, or to order additional resources, call toll free 888–566–9949 (KNOW WHY), or visit **www.MyCrossCulture.com** and go to the Resource section.

- ❑ Contact your pastor or church staff to encourage a church wide launch of the entire family of product.

- ❑ Contact your pastor or church staff to arrange for the celebration that concludes this course (Session 8) to be presented before the entire church. The timing and venue for this event will, of course, need to be coordinated with other staff, included in the church calendar, and promoted in church bulletins, newsletters, websites, etc.

- ❑ Carefully and completely review this *True or False* **Leaders Guide** and the *True or False Workbook*.

- ❑ Pray that this course will be instrumental in inciting a spiritual revolution within your church, school, home, or camp.

Administration of the True or False Course

By Cindy Ann Pitts

True or False is an eight-week course designed to teach children the Bible's "Big Truths" about having a personal relationship with God. Combined with the other *Beyond Belief* resources, the entire church body can be equipped to reinforce the basic biblical truth about salvation. Of course, True or False is adaptable and can be used at various times. Consider these ideas:

- Summer Sunday school session
- Backyard Bible club
- Children's Apartment Ministry
- Children's day camp
- Sunday or Wednesday evening children's programs
- Church cell-group nights
- After-school childcare
- Children's worship
- Children's camp–For a four-to-five-day camp, use sessions 1, 3, 5, and 7 for the daily small-group Bible studies. The camp pastor can preach/teach the content from sessions 2, 4, and 6 as the sermons for the evening worship services. Children can do the application sections and complete the work-book pages for sessions 2, 4, and 6 during the evening devotionals in their small groups. Session 8's drama can be performed at a final awards and review time. The wonderful thing about a camp setting is that the children can start and finish all eight sessions because they are all there.
- Whenever you want to share the Good News with children!

Select Leadership

As you seek leadership, consider persons in your church who work with children regularly and effectively. Schoolteachers, counselors, Sunday school teachers, and social workers in your church may enjoy the opportunity to share their skills with children in this way.

There are three basic positions of leadership for this teaching plan:

- *True or False* **Program Coordinator** – This person will oversee the entire course.
- *True or False* **Study Group Leader** – This person will direct the work of

one group of children. A group can consist of one to twenty-five children. The study group leader is responsible for planning the hour's session and leading the Gear Up for the Truth time as well as the Teach the Truth time. This person may also teach a small group during the "Apply the Truth to Life" time if you cannot secure enough leadership. This person may also be referred to as the lead teacher.

- ***True or False* Small-Group Leaders** – This person will lead a group of six to eight children in small-group activities that relate to the Bible truths presented through the Teach the Truth time. In the small discussion group the children will be challenged to apply the day's Big Truth to their own lives. They will work in the student workbook and guide children toward biblical truth.

Enlist teachers who are confident of their salvation experience. This course is a study of how a person becomes a Christian. As you enlist leadership, ask them to share with you when and how they came to place their faith in Jesus Christ. It would be a disservice to children to have people teach this material who are not passionate about their own salvation and spiritual growth. Seek out teachers who sense that God is leading them to undertake this ministry and who feel comfortable sharing the gospel with children. Naturally you will also want to look for teachers who enjoy being with children and whom children enjoy being around.

Prior to enlisting anyone for the responsibilities listed above, follow the procedures set by your church for enlisting church members to work with children.

The program coordinator will be expected to:

- Enlist enough study group leaders and small-group leaders for the expected number of children.
- Provide materials and information to the leaders and teachers.
- Design publicity to encourage parents to bring their children to the series.
- Enroll children and assign them to a group.
- Purchase and distribute materials and supplies needed to teach the course.
- Secure the dates for the True or False Sessions on the church calendar.
- Schedule rooms that will be used for the learning sessions.
- Communicate with parents and teachers.
- Follow up with children who have made decisions to become Christians.

(The program coordinator may also serve as a study group leader and discussion group leader.)

Study group leaders are expected to:

- Plan each of the eight sessions in detail for a group of children.

- Divide the children into small discussion groups of six to eight children and assign them a small-group leader.

- Lead the Gear Up for the Truth introductory activity.

- Lead the Teach the Truth time.

Small-group leaders are expected to:

- Assist the study group leader with the Gear Up for the Truth activity.

- Lead the "Apply the Truth to Life" time.

- Lead children in discussion as they work through the activities in the workbook.

It would be beneficial for all the leadership listed above to read *Beyond Belief to Convictions* by Josh McDowell. All the leadership must be committed to preparation and to prayer for the children participating in this study.

Determine Group Structure

Create a group for every twenty-five children who pre-register. While it is possible to teach all children, grades one through six, together, it would be best to closely age-grade your groups. But even if you have all the children in one group for your Teach the Truth time, you can still divide the groups by age for the smaller "Apply the Truth to Life" time. The small discussion groups should be formed for every six to eight children. The ideal group size for children's discussion groups is six. Small groups allow for each child to actively participate.

Assign Leaders to Each Group

Assign at least two adult teachers to each group. We suggest two adults because:

- Adult teachers can share preparation responsibilities.

- Adult teachers can review together their impressions of the learning of the group.

- In the event of a problem, one adult can work on the problem while the other is free to keep leading the group. For example, if a child becomes sick or a discipline problem arises, one adult leader could give the child the time he needs.

Purchase Resources

You will need to purchase the products listed below:

- *True or False Leaders Guide.* This is the Leaders Guide you are reading right now! You will need one of these for each of your adult teachers. This guide has four sections. The Introduction describes the Children's True or False course and the Beyond Belief emphasis. The Administration section (you are reading right now) helps you to administer the program and guide volunteers to become effective group leaders. The Parent section consists of reproducible pages for the parent information packets. The Lesson Plan section contains detailed lesson plans for teaching the eight True or False sessions with children.

- *True or False Younger Children's Workbook.* You will need one of these workbooks for each younger child enrolled. This activity book is specifically designed for first through third graders.

- *True or False Older Children's Workbook.* This activity workbook is designed for fourth through sixth graders. You will need to purchase one for each older child you expect in your group.

These two children's activity books will be used during each session. The activities contained in them help stimulate discussion. Each child's activity book should remain with the adult leaders until the end of session 8. After the last session, the children may keep their workbooks to remind them of the Big Truths they have learned.

To order your workbook and other **Beyond Belief** resources, see pages 25–28 or visit **www.MyCrossCulture.com** and go to the Resource section.

Adapting this Course to Meet the Needs of Children

Study the children you will be teaching. Remind yourself that we should teach children the material, and not teach material to children. Did that sound confusing? To teach life-changing Bible studies, the emphasis must be on the lives of children. As you get to know your students, you might need to adapt the material to best meet their needs. For example, if you are working with a churched group or are teaching in a Christian school, you may discover that all the children in your group have already trusted Christ. If so, use this workbook to teach witnessing skills and to further ground them in the truth. Guide them to discuss how they would use the Bible verses and Big Truths to help lead someone to Christ.

If you are teaching in an outreach situation where children have not had much exposure to the Bible, you might consider going slower and adding more sessions. If the children can do the workbook activities independently, encourage them to do so.

True or False

Work item–by–item with children who cannot complete the workbooks on their own. While the *Younger Children's Workbook* is designed for children in first through third grades, you might feel that your third graders can easily master the *Older Children's Workbook*. Purchase the workbook that suits your group best.

If you are teaching first through sixth graders in the same large group, it will still work best for you to have both *Older* and *Younger Children's Workbooks* in the same room. The leaders guide is written with suggestions throughout on how to adapt for younger children. Often the workbook pages for the younger child are simplified versions of the same activities for the older child. This was done because many ministries include multiple age groups in learning situations.

Teach to the top! When you have many learning levels in the same group, always teach to stretch and challenge the children who have more knowledge and abilities. Then use these children to help teach the other children. Children learn well from other children. As you teach to challenge the top students in the large-group time, the others will gain so much more. In the small-group time you can specifically enlist some children in advance to help others as they work in pairs to complete the workbook activities. Children who help will reinforce their own learning by teaching and will experience the joy of serving.

A Note on Visual Aids

In the lesson plans, you will be instructed in the Prepare sections to make visual aids. That term was used instead of listing only one way to teach visually. If you are comfortable with creating Power Point presentations and you have access to a Power Point projector, the children will enjoy the use of the computer-generated visual aids. However, you can create the same information on an overhead projector or on poster board.

Schedule the Sessions

Set a time, date, and place for the *True or False* sessions. If your church is conducting a church–wide Beyond Belief emphasis, then your group will meet concurrently with the adult, college, and youth groups. Otherwise, select any eight-week period in the life of your church that will be conducive to consistent attendance.

The best place for the *True or False* sessions will be rooms that are designated for children and have the appropriate child-sized furniture. During the Teach the Truth time, children will be seated in a semicircle around the study group leader. During the "Apply the Truth to Life" time, children should be seated around tables since they will be using their workbooks. They should also be facing each other so that good discussion can take place.

Promote the True or False Course

Good ways to promote the course include:

- Articles in the church paper or newsletter.
- A letter to the parents of all children on your roll and in your prospect file.
- Announcements in the parents' Sunday school classes.
- Direct calling or e-mailing to all parents whose children are enrolled in your church programs. If your church has a phone tree, use it!
- Articles in the local papers.
- Announcements made on local radio stations.
- Child-oriented businesses will often allow you to place your posters and flyers in places where parents and children frequent.

Conduct Leadership Training

As you recruit adults to assist you in teaching *True or False*, give them a leaders guide and a workbook so they can begin reviewing them. Before the course begins, each teacher accepting a position should read through all the sessions. This will familiarize them with the materials they will be using and the supplies they will need. Being acquainted with the overall content of the book and each session will help them later when they prepare in detail for the session they will be leading next.

After each teacher has had the opportunity to read a *True or False Leaders Guide,* and the *True or False Children's Workbooks,* conduct your leadership-training meeting. Overview the course, and answer any questions your teachers might have. Give your teachers the big picture view of the *True or False* course. Make a list of the children you hope will attend the program and ask your teachers to pray daily for them and their families.

Impress on your leadership the importance of the *True or False* course in helping children develop a relationship with God. Help them catch a vision of how important it is to help children place their faith in Jesus Christ for the forgiveness of their sin. Assure them that many children who have already become Christians do not fully understand the Big Truths we will be teaching. Help them to grasp that they are assisting parents in their vital responsibility to pass on biblical values to the next generation.

Devote time in your training to discuss with your teachers how they feel concerning leading children to Christ. Find out if they are comfortable talking with children individually about salvation. Many adults feel comfortable witnessing to other adults but not to children. The following points may help you as you teach the teachers.

Children and Salvation

God is at work in the lives of first-grade through sixth-grade children. At some point during these years, most children become aware that their sin separates them from God. As we work with this age group we must be sure that our evangelistic efforts are both intentional and age appropriate.

A relationship with God is a supernatural miracle. Just as the Spirit of God works in the hearts and minds of adults and leads them to Christ, so does he in the lives of children. Children–no less than adults–can become Christians when God's Holy Spirit leads them to make that decision.

There is only one plan of salvation. God does not offer an easy plan for children and a harder one for adults. But in many ways it is easier for children to trust Christ, and there are many advantages for people to come to Christ early in life. Consider these thoughts:

- *Children are more tenderhearted and trusting.* The simplicity of the gospel can be a stumbling block for adults, but children simply trust that Jesus forgives them. They do not question that God could love them, as many adults do.

- *Children are humble.* Pride often keeps youth and adults from agreeing with God that they have sinned and have a need for a Savior.

- *Children's lives are less cluttered.* Adults are often too distracted to take time to consider the claims of Christ.

- *Children believe readily.* Adults have learned to doubt; their life experiences sometimes make them slow to believe. Children, however, are less jaded; they are often more quick to trust God.

- *Children's lives have not yet been complicated by their past.* Children do not have a lifetime of sin to overcome. Many guilt-ridden adults have a hard enough time forgiving themselves, and they just cannot believe God will forgive them.

Here are some things to keep in mind when talking to children about becoming a Christian:

1. **Counsel children individually.** Talk to children individually after class. Contact the parents to let them know about their child's decision. When possible, meet with the parents as you talk with their child. This is a life-changing conversation. Christian parents will want to be present. Lost parents need to hear the Good News. I have led many parents to pray to receive Christ right after their child has just prayed. It is a tender moment in the life of parents when they witness their child making such an impor-

tant commitment and they are most sensitive at that moment to the Holy Spirit.

2. **_Be conversational._** Often when adults talk with children, the conversation sounds like a monologue. They tend to talk to not with the child. To help:

   - Ask children if they like to read. If so, let them read the Scripture passages.
   - Invite the children to participate, supplying as much information as they can. This is a great way to discover what the children already know. Some children have given me the entire plan of salvation as I guided them through the questions. Gently correct misinformation.

3. **_Ask open-ended questions._** For example, "Joseph, why do you want to become a Christian?" Or, "Christina, why do you think a person needs to become a Christian?" Open-ended questions require the child to think. Children must give you an answer other than yes or no. Often when adults ask a child a yes or no question, they unconsciously answer the question for them with their body language, such as a nod of the head to indicate yes. Toward the end of the conversation, at the time of commitment, you will use some yes and no questions, but at that point the questions are simply to confirm what the child has already told you.

4. **_Give children time to think._** Adults are not comfortable with silence. When children are asked questions, they often need time to think. Wait for the answers.

5. **_Listen carefully to children's questions and answers._** The insight you gain from the responses will guide you as you continue the conversation and help you know if they understand the information.

6. **_Use the Bible._** The Bible gives authority to what you say. As you use your Bible, you model for children how to use it. Use five to six key verses, if possible, from the child's Bible. Too many Scripture verses could overwhelm and distract the child.

7. **_Show sincere concern, but avoid becoming emotional._** Children are easily influenced emotionally. They are eager to please adults. If you become teary-eyed, you will confuse them. Most children still associate tears with negative emotions.

8. **_Avoid talking about sin in such a way that you invade the children's pri-_**

vacy or elicit an unhealthy sense of condemnation. Children can easily feel condemned. Just because they agree they have lied does not necessarily mean we should relate their sin to rebellion against God. Be sensitive to the tender and immature nature of a child's heart.

Communicate with Parents

It is increasingly difficult to get parents to attend meetings. To keep parents aware, prepare an information packet for each set of parents. The information for the packet is included on pages 21, 22, 130 and 131. You have permission to reproduce all the sheets for your True or False Parent Information Packet. The packet is designed to help parents understand the major concepts their children will learn in their True or False study group. They will be given the memory verses and encouraged to help their children learn and review the Scripture.

Pray As You Prepare

Pray for yourself as you prepare. Ask God to guide you as you present his truth to the very best of your ability for his own honor. Ask God to bless you with creativity and patience.

Pray for the children you teach and their families. The battle for the hearts and minds of your children is not primarily an educational battle–it is a spiritual battle. When you teach the Big Truths, you are not simply addressing an educational issue, you are presenting the truth that God sent Jesus to have a relationship with each of your children.

Evaluate Your Progress and Remain Flexible

As you evaluate the progress of your groups, you might need to make changes. Prayerfully keep in mind what is in the best interest of the children. For example, if more children come to session 1 than you had planned, praise the Lord! Then do all you can to provide more leadership and create more groups by session 2.

PARENTS' INFORMATION- This page may be adapted and reproduced.

Dear [Parents' Names]:

We live in a culture that is influencing our children to create their own religious beliefs based more on what they think than what the Bible teaches. The message they receive from even some adults around them is that every religion is right. They are introduced to many lies in our society; one being that there are many ways to get to know God.

We want to help you teach your child to spot the lies the culture promotes. For that reason, we have chosen to offer the *True or False* material in the church. It is a part of the *Beyond Belief to Convictions* campaign launched by John McDowell.

In our church the *True or False* session will be taught on [day of the week] at [time] in the [place]. This study is open to all children in grades one through six. We have enlisted excellent children's workers to help guide your child through each of the Bible's Big Truths. [If you are able to have age-graded groups, parents would like to know, so in this space you might say that there will be six classes offered, one for each grade. Add a sentence to explain your groups and provide the teachers' names.]

Use these ideas to reinforce the teaching at home:

• Look over the Big Truths with the motions and practice them with your child. Also in our study we want to help the children identify the lies around them.

• Display the Bible Verse to Know sheet and think of ways to teach the verse to your child at home. Memorize each verse along with your child.

• Do all in your power to see that your child is present for all eight sessions.

• Pray for your child. If your child has not yet made a personal commitment to Christ, pray that during these classes, the Holy Spirit will speak to his or her heart.

• Read Beyond Belief to Convictions by Josh McDowell. We will have this book available to purchase or you may borrow a copy from the church library.

If you have any questions, please call me at [your phone number]. I hope to see your child on [date, time and place].

Sincerely,

[Your name and position]

Permission is granted to duplicate this page for parents

SESSION THEMES
THE BIG TRUTHS/THE WORLD'S BIG LIES

SESSION 1: CREATED FOR GOD

> Big Truth: God created me to be his friend.
> Big Lie: I don't need God's friendship.

SESSION 2: WHAT SIN DOES TO MY FRIENDSHIP WITH GOD

> Big Truth: God is holy and takes my sin seriously.
> Big Lie: I can decide what is right or wrong for me.

SESSION 3: LOST AND ALONE BECAUSE OF SIN

> Big Truth: Sin separates me from God.
> Big Lie: I can live my life my way.

SESSION 4: JESUS IS THE ONE AND ONLY SAVIOR

> Big Truth: God sent Jesus to be the Savior of the world.
> Big Lie: There are a lot of ways to get to know God.

SESSION 5: I CAN BE FORGIVEN

> Big Truth: God planned for Jesus to pay the price for our sins.
> Big Lie: I am a good person–I can please God.

SESSION 6: I CAN BE SURE JESUS WILL ALWAYS LOVE ME

> Big Truth: Jesus will never leave me.
> Big Lie: I must work hard to please God on my own.

SESSION 7: GROWING UP IN GOD'S FAMILY

> Big Truth: When I trust in Jesus, God makes me his child.
> Big Lie: God and the church are fine–when I have the time.

SESSION 8: CELEBRATE

> Big Truth: God celebrates when I come back to him.
> (No Big Lie for session 8)

Permission is granted to duplicate this page for parents

THE BIG TRUTHS

Session 1

God created me to be his friend.

Stand up and clasp
hands together, like a hand shake.

Session 2

God is holy and takes my sin seriously.

Use arms and hands to make
an X across the face.

Session 3

Sin separates me from God.

With arms extended forward in front of
their body, hands flexed with fingers
pointed upward, take two steps back..

Session 4

God sent Jesus to be the Savior of the world.

Touch palm of right hand with the middle
finger of left hand, then repeat the gesture
with opposite hands, as in the sign language
symbol for Jesus, and point to heaven.

Permission is granted to duplicate this page for parents

True or False

THE BIG TRUTHS

Session 5

God planned for Jesus to pay the price for my sins.

Cross hands over face again as in Truth 2; but then break arms apart and reach up to God like a child who wants to be held reaches up to his father.

Session 6

Jesus will never leave me.

Hug yourself with arms wrapped around body.

Session 7

When I trust in Jesus, God makes me his child.

Form arms as if rocking a baby.

Session 8

God celebrates when I come back to him.

Begin by clapping hands then raise arms, palms up and hands raised to God.

Permission is granted to duplicate this page for parents

BELIEF.

Incite A CROSSCULTURE™ Revolution

Here is a foundational family of products to transform a generation into passionate followers of Christ who know why they believe what they believe.

BE CONVINCED OF WHY YOU BELIEVE

Beyond Belief to Convictions Book to Adults

Having Christian convictions means being so thoroughly convinced that Christ and his Word are both objectively true and relationally meaningful that you act on your beliefs regardless of the consequences. *Beyond Belief* contains the blueprint for a revolution in the lives of young people. It will help you lead them to a real encounter with God and transform them into passionate followers of Christ. ***Beyond Belief to Convictions*** 0-8423-7409-4

The CrossCulture Revolution Book to Adults

Why call for a revolution? Josh and Ron cite at least three compelling reasons: (1) Despite the efforts of the church, Christian schools, and Christian families, the vast majority of our kids lead lives virtually no different than non-Christians; (2) they consistently make wrong moral choices; and (3) upon leaving home our young people do not remain in the church. The authors offer a spiritual revolution manifesto for the church and family to raise up a cross culture—a transformed generation of passionate followers of Christ. ***The CrossCulture Revolution*** 0-8423-7976-2

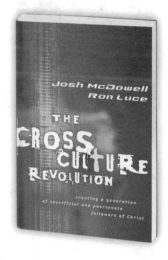

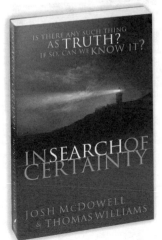

In Search of Certainty Book to Adults

Statistics are alarming. Eighty-eight percent of the U.S. population does not believe in a moral absolute. Postmodernism has undermined the concept of absolute truth in the past generation, leaving even Christians groping for meaning and certainty in their lives. This book exposes the irrationalities of atheistic positions, showing that God is real and truth is absolute, and only trust in him can provide certainty that life has meaning and fulfillment. An excellent book to give to a seeker friend.
In Search of Certainty 0-8423-7972-X

Begin Your CROSSCULTURE™ Revolution at www.BeyondBelief.com

BE CONVINCED OF WHY YOU BELIEVE

Josh McDowell's Youth Devotions 2
Josh McDowell's Family Devotions 2
to Youth/Families

"We are not fighting against people made of flesh and blood, but against the evil rulers and authorities of the unseen world . . ." (Ephesians 6:12, NLT). More than ever our young people need a spiritual defense. This second installment of Josh's best-selling youth and family devotions offers two 365–daily devotional encounters with the true Power Source to strengthen your family spiritually and provide your young people with a resource that will help them combat today's culture. *Josh McDowell's Youth Devotions 2* 0-8423-4096-3 *Josh McDowell's Family Devotions 2* 0-8423-5625-8

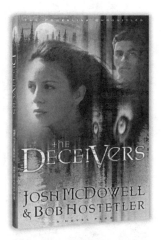

The Deceivers **Book to Youth**

Written in the popular NovelPlus format, this book combines the adventures of Sarah Milford and Ryan Ortiz and their search for meaning, along with Josh's insights found in sections called "The Inside Story."

In dramatic fashion *The Deceivers* explains that unless Christ is who he claims to be—the true Son of God—then his offer to redeem us and provide meaning to life can't be real. This book presents not only the compelling evidence for the deity of Christ, but also how God's plan is to transform us into a new creature with an intimate relationship with him. *The Deceivers* 0-8423-7969-X

Children Demand a Verdict **Book to Children**

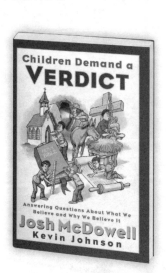

Children need clear and direct answers to their questions about God, the Bible, sin, death, etc. Directed to children ages 7–11 this question and answer book tackles 77 tough issues with clarity and relevance, questions such as: Why did God make people? How do we know Jesus was God? How could God write a book? Is the Bible always right? Are parts of the Bible make believe? Why did Jesus die? Did Jesus really come back to life? Does God always forgive me? Why do people die? Will I come back to life like Jesus? *Children Demand a Verdict* 0-8423-7971-1

BE COMMITTED TO WHAT YOU BELIEVE

Video Series for Adult Groups

This five-part interactive video series features Josh McDowell sharing how your young people have adopted distorted beliefs about God, truth, and reality and what you as adults can do about it. Step by step he explains how to lead your kids to know "why we believe what we believe" and how that is truly relevant to their everyday lives. This series provides the perfect launch for your group to build the true foundation of Christianity in the lives of the family, beginning with adults.

The series includes five video sessions of approximately 25 minutes each, a comprehensive Leader's Guide with reproducible handouts, the *Beyond Belief to Convictions* book, and a complimentary copy of *The Deceivers* book. (Also available on DVD.)

Belief Matters Video Series 0-8423-8018-3

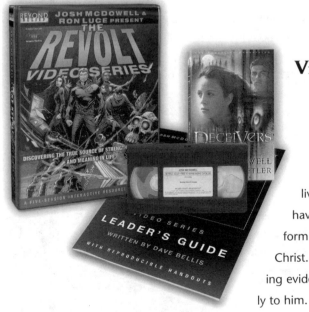

Video Series for Youth Groups

Combining a powerful message, compelling video illustrations, and captivating group activities this series will enable you to lead your students to this convincing conclusion: the ways of the world do not produce true meaning in life—only Christ as the true Son of God can transform our "dead lives" into a dynamic and meaningful life in relationship with him. Josh and Ron have created this interactive series to incite a revolution—a revolution to transform your young people into a generation of sacrificial and passionate followers of Christ. As a foundational building block of Christianity this series offers overwhelming evidence that Christ is the Messiah and challenges each student to commit totally to him.

The series includes five dramatic video illustrations, Leader's Guide of teaching lessons with reproducible handouts for group activities, and *The Deceivers* NovelPlus book. (Also available on DVD.) **The Revolt Video Series** 0-8423-8016-7

Begin Your **CROSSCULTURE**™ Revolution at www.BeyondBelief.com

BELIEF®

BE CHANGED BY WHO YOU BELIEVE

Workbook for Adult Groups

Combining interactive group discussion with daily activities, this workbook helps you overcome the distorted views of Christ and biblical truth held by most children and youth today. It will help you lead them to a fresh encounter with the "God who is passionate about his relationship with you" (Exodus 34:14, NLT). The daily activities reveal a credible, real, and relevant Christ you can share with each family member.

The workbook study provides eight solid group teaching sessions for the weekly at-home-assignments to model the message before others.

Belief Matters Workbook Wkbk: 0-8423-8010-8   Ld. Gd: 0-8423-8011-6

Workbook for Youth Groups

When your students reject the world's counterfeit way of life, what will life in Christ really be like for them? This 8-session course helps each of your students realize that new life in Christ is about transformation, about belonging to Christ and one another in his Body, about knowing who they really are, and about living out their mission in life.

The Revolt Workbook is an 8-session youth group interactive course followed up with students engaging in two daily exercises per week. This study is the perfect follow-up to the companion *Revolt Video Series*. ***The Revolt Workbook*** Wkbk: 0-8423-7978-9 Ld. Gd: 0-8423-7979-7

Workbook for Children's Groups

To raise up the next generation of committed followers of Christ, we must start when they are young. These workbooks for children grades 1–3 and grades 4–6 present the foundational truth of why Christ came to earth. Written in simple terms, it leads your children to realize why doing wrong has separated them from God and why only Christ can transform them into a close family relationship with God.

In eight fun-filled sessions, your children will learn why Christ is the true way and all other ways are false. These sessions lead children to a loving encounter with the "God who is passionate about his relationship with [them]" (Exodus 34:14, NLT).

True or False Workbook Younger Wkbk: 0-8423-8012-4 Older Wkbk: 0-8423-8013-2 Ld. Gd: 0-8423-8014-0

**Contact your Christian Supplier to obtain these resources
and begin the revolution in your home, church, and community.**

TRUE OR FALSE SESSIONS

DETERMINING WHAT WE BELIEVE AND WHY WE BELIEVE IT

True or False

**God created me
to be his friend.**

Stand up and clasp
hands together, like a
hand shake.

SESSION 1
CREATED FOR GOD

SESSION GOALS:
As a result of this session children should be able to:
- Understand God made them for a personal friendship with himself.
- Believe a relationship with God is what provides meaning for our lives.
- Learn that God is passionate about them.
- Have a desire to know God.

TODAY'S BIG TRUTH: God created me to be his friend.

THE WORLD'S BIG LIE: I don't need God's friendship.

KEY SCRIPTURES FOR TODAY'S SESSION:
Genesis 1–2   Creation
Genesis 1:27; Genesis 2:7; Psalm 139:1-18

MEMORY VERSE: Exodus 34:14

Older Children:
"You must worship no other gods, but only the LORD, for he is a God who is passionate about his relationship with you."

Younger Children
"God who is passionate about his relationship with you."

LEADERS NEED TO KNOW

At its core, the Christian faith is about a relationship with God. That is what provides true meaning to all of our lives. Everything that Scripture teaches us to believe, to be, and to do contains one common thread: an intimate, real relationship with the one true God of the universe.

Children can be taught that God created us and that he created us for a relationship–a friendship with him. It is very important that as you talk to children about a friendship with God that you do not minimize the awesome holiness of God. A friendship with God is not a friendship of equals.

From birth, a person embarks on an adventure of self-discovery. It is a baby's developmental milestone to "find" their fingers and toes, to respond to their own name, and to discover that people and objects continue to exist even if baby cannot see them. In all these activities, the infant is asking, "Who am I?" even before the question can be voiced. You can help children answer that question by teaching them that they are a special creation of God. When children, and all people for that matter, believe that they are a special creation of God it will affect their behavior. Understanding that we are God's creation will give us self-worth and we will be able to view ourselves as worthy of the respect of others. Understanding that other people are a part of God's creation will help us value and respect them. But even more important, understanding that we were created for a relationship with God demands that we each respond to God. We each must accept or reject a relationship with him.

The first Big Truth we want to teach children is that ***God created me to be his friend.*** This truth answers the question, "Who am I?" It causes us to have to decide if we will be a friend of God or pursue our own selfish desires. Our culture influences us to believe individuals are in control of their own lives, independent from God. The Big Lie we are taught is "I don't need God's friendship." In a culture that teaches us that we can expect to "have it our way," submitting to God sounds unnecessary. We must teach children to spot the lie and respond to the truth.

Teach the children that God's original plan was that we would enjoy life like the one he designed for Adam and Eve in the Garden of Eden. He created us for an intimate friendship with himself. We were designed to walk with God in the garden. Speak lovingly of God and you will be able to lead children to love him.

GEAR UP FOR THE TRUTH
(10 MINUTES)

PREPARE
❏ Attach a long piece of craft paper to one wall of the classroom; if possible make it the length of the wall.
❏ If you have not already done so, be sure to contact your pastor or church staff to make arrangements for the celebration that concludes this course (Session 8).

PROVIDE
❏ A roll of craft paper
❏ Washable, broad-tipped felt markers in a variety of colors–at least 2–3 per child

Since this is your first *True or False* session, make sure the children in your group know each other. Adult leaders should arrive totally prepared to teach at least 20 minutes before the children arrive so that you can focus on greeting each child as he arrives and helping each child feel special and a part of the group.

1. GET ACQUAINTED AND INVOLVE YOUR EARLY ARRIVERS
Help early arrivers get acquainted through the use of a few non-threatening questions. Here are some examples:
  • Where do you go to school?
  • How many people are in your family at home? How are they related to you?
  • What do you think is the most beautiful thing God created?

Be sure to share this and more information about yourself.

2. BEST FRIENDS GRAFFITI WALL
On one wall of your classroom, attach a large sheet of craft paper, the whole length of the wall if possible. Instruct the children to go to the wall and, using colored felt-tipped markers, write words or draw symbols or pictures that would illustrate the answer to the following questions:
  • What do friends do together?
  • What makes a person a good friend?
  • How do you become friends with someone?

Give the children about 5–8 minutes to work on their word art, and then discuss their answers. **Say**: "We are going to discover that God wants to have a friend-ship with us."

TEACH THE TRUTH

(25 MINUTES)

PREPARE

❑ For activity 4, using either a dry-erase board or poster board, write at the top: "Made in God's Image, but We Are Not God." Under the title make two columns. Label one "God" and the other "People." As you teach the activity, write down differences between God and people.

❑ Posters of "How I Reflect my Designer." Make 11 x 14 posters of the six statements in activity 5, either hand-made or computer-generated.

❑ Large copy of Psalm 139:1–18, using Power Point, poster board, or overhead transparencies.

PROVIDE

❑ Bibles
❑ Large sheets of white paper; washable markers
❑ Dry-erase board; dry-erase markers
❑ Optional: Teaching pictures of days of Creation; tacks or tape
❑ Optional: Sidewalk chalk for outdoors

1. STUDY THE BIBLE

Guide the children to open their Bibles to Genesis 1. Provide Bibles for children who did not bring one. Teachers need to assist children who are not familiar with finding the passages in the Bible to find the scripture that will be studied. Help children feel comfortable using the Bible.

While the children keep their Bibles open to Genesis 1, briefly review the Creation story. The emphasis for today's session is not to teach Creation, but to point to the fact that God created only people for a relationship with himself. Teach from your open Bible. Include these facts on the days of creation:
  • Day 1 – God created day and night (1:3–5).
  • Day 2 – God created the sky (1:6–8).
  • Day 3 – God created the land and seas, plants and trees (1:9–12).
  • Day 4 – God created the sun, moon and stars (1:14–18).
  • Day 5 – God created the sea creatures and birds (1:20–23).
  • Day 6 – God created the land animals and HUMANS (1:24–27).

If your children's ministry has sets of biblical teaching pictures, you may choose to present this material with the pictures depicting the days of Creation mounted on the wall.

2. FOCUS ON GENESIS 1:26 AND GENESIS 2:7

Say: "God made the earth, sky, seas, then the sun, moon, and stars. He made green plants and trees that produced food to eat. God then created a great variety of animals. It would seem like his universe was complete, but on that sixth day, when the whole world was ready, God made his greatest creation. He decided to make something that was like him is some ways. Let's read about it in the Bible."

Read Genesis 1:26: "Then God said, 'Let us make people in our image, to be like ourselves. They will be masters over all life––the fish in the sea, the birds in the sky, and all the livestock, wild animals, and small animals.'"

Ask: "What does the Bible tell us is God's most important creation?" Hopefully, the children will answer that people are God's most important creation. If not, guide them in that direction. Our creation was different than the creation of everything else God made. All the other things God made, God just spoke into being. When God created people, what did he do differently?" (Made people in his own image.)

3. TRACE SHADOW IMAGES

If it is possible to go outdoors, and if it is a sunny day, use the following activity to illustrate what the word *image* means. If you cannot go outdoors, with a bright light you can create a silhouette of a child on a large piece of white paper, then trace around the silhouette with a marker.

If outdoors, pair off the children and ask them to take turns tracing out each other's shadows. They will enjoy using sidewalk chalk to trace their shadows, or you may simply want them to observe their shadows and not even trace them.

Say: "In a simple way, these shadows represent your image. They reflect your shape–at least today! The Bible says we were made in the image of God. In our session today we are going to read and discover what that means."

4. MADE IN GOD'S IMAGE, BUT WE ARE NOT GOD!

Say: "What do you think the Bible means when it says that man was created in God's own image?" Listen to their responses.

Call attention to the chart you have made on the marker board or on the poster board: "Made in God's Image, but We Are Not God!" (see "Prepare," above). Help children understand that being made in the image of God does not mean that we are, or could ever become, God.

To guide the children to identify the natures of God and people, **ask**:
- When is God's birthday?
- When is your birthday? *(Point out that we are not eternal like God.)*
- Can God create something from nothing?
- Can you create something from nothing?

  (Point out that we are not creative like God. While people can make things from existing items and can think creatively, we cannot create something from nothing.)
- Does God know all things?
- Do you know everything about all things?

  (Point out that we are not all-knowing like God.)

As children make comments, write those characteristics of God and people on your chart. Challenge the children to continue to think of ways that God and people are different.

Children may say: being able to love unconditionally, forgive completely, awesome, and all-powerful. Mature children may say: omniscient, omnipresent, omnipotent, or highest authority.

5. HOW I REFLECT MY DESIGNER

Say: "We've learned how we are different from God. However, being made in God's image means we are like God in some ways. It is because of these abilities that I can have a friendship with God." Hold the 11 x 14 posters of the following six statements you made before class. As you teach, walk around the room and post each of the statements on the wall. As you discuss each one, point out how only God and people have the following abilities.

I am like God because…
1. I can **talk** with God.
2. I can **know** right from wrong.
3. I can make **choices**.
4. I can **think** and **plan**.
5. I can **communicate** with other people.
6. I can **love** God and others.

Work these concepts into your discussion.
- People are the highest of all of God's creations. We are important to God and that is why he gave us the mental and spiritual qualities we would need to have a friendship with him.
- Our pets, as much as we love them, do not have spiritual qualities like people.
- Because we are made in God's image, our life is sacred to God. That is why murder is sin; God values human life. That is why even hurting people's feelings is wrong. When we insult or harm another person, we are harming the image that God gave us.

6. BECAUSE GOD IS LOVE

Guide the children to recall some of the words and thoughts expressed on the "graffiti wall" concerning friendship.

Say: "It really sounds amazing to think that the awesome Creator of the whole universe would want to have a personal friendship with us. But that is exactly what the Bible teaches us. Let's see this truth in the Bible for ourselves. The Bible says God knows us, thinks about us, and loves us. Let's read Psalm 139. The writer David loved God and knew God's love and friendship."

Project or show your copy of Psalm 139:1–18. If you have older children, you may want to use all 18 verses and allow volunteers to read them aloud. For younger children, use only verses 1–4 and 17–18 and read to them.

Have the children to point out words or phrases that show that the writer of these words really believed that God knew him and wanted to have a friendship with him.

7. TODAY'S BIG TRUTHS

Say: "God wants us to be friends with him. Through the next seven weeks we are going to learn what we need to know to develop our friendship with God. To help us do that we're going to learn what we'll call the 'Big Truths.' The actions to go along with them will help you remember them." Go through the motions one by one.

To teach the Big Truths, refer to the list below (or see the Big Truths with illustrations on 116 of this leaders guide).

Big Truth 1:   God created me to be his friend.
                    Expression: Stand up and clasp hands together.

Big Truth 2:   God is holy and takes my sin seriously.
                    Expression: Use arms and hands to make an X across the face.

Big Truth: 3   Sin Separates me from God.
                    Expression: With arms extended forward in front of their body, hands flexed with fingers pointed upward take two steps back (Motion as if pushing away).

Big Truth 4:   God sent Jesus to be the Savior of the world.
                    Expression: Touch palms of hands alternately with the middle fingers, as in the sign language symbol for Jesus, and then point to heaven.

Big Truth 5:   God planned for Jesus to pay the price for my sins.
                    Expression: Cross hands over face again as in Truth 2; but then break arms apart and reach up to God like a child who wants to be held reaches up to their father.

Big Truth 6:   Jesus will never leave me.
                    Expression: Hug self with arms wrapped around.

Big Truth 7:   When I trust in Jesus, God makes me his child.
                    Expression: Form arms as if rocking a baby.

Big Truth 8:   God celebrates when I come back to him.
                    Expression: Begin by clapping hands, then raise arms, palms up, and hands raised toward God.

8. INTRODUCE THE CHILDREN TO THEIR SMALL GROUP

Divide into small groups for discussion time. **Say:** "We are going to break into discussion groups. You will be in the same group for the next seven weeks. Your group will do some fun activities and talk about how we can be friends with God." Divide the children by age into groups. For the best interaction, limit groups to six to eight children. Each group must have its own adult leader.

9. PRAY

Guide the children to pray silently with these statements:

• Praise God for something about yourself that you like.

• Thank God for giving you the gift of life.

• Ask God to help you in some specific way.

APPLY THE TRUTH TO LIFE

(25 MINUTES–SMALL-GROUP TIME)

PROVIDE

❑ *True or False* children's workbooks
❑ Pens, pencils, or thin felt-tipped markers

1. WELCOME CHILDREN TO YOUR GROUP

Welcome each child placed in your group and continue the process of getting acquainted.

As a small group leader, begin on the right track with children by helping them find their positive space in the group. Introduce the children to their *True or False Workbooks*. Point out the pages with the eight Big Truths they talked about earlier and will learn during the next few weeks. Ask the children to turn to the memory verse chart in their book. **Say:** "Over the next eight weeks, I want to challenge you to memorize some great Bible verses. When you can say your verses by memory to a teacher, you will get a sticker to place in the box next to the verse on this page!"

Teachers, children have various abilities to memorize. It's important not to compare children with such things as incentive charts for all the children to see who has memorized scriptures and who has not. The personal incentive chart in their workbooks will be sufficient motivation and reward for those children who can and will memorize these scriptures.

True or False

2. WHOM DO YOU SEE? (Workbook page 5)

Give each child a *True or False Workbook*. The first activity on page 5 will help them to discover they are God's special creation. As they share with the group their answers, it will also help members of the group get better acquainted.

Guide children to reflect on themselves as they work through the "Whom Do You See?" activity. Tell the children to answer the questions honestly, and that they do not have to share their answers. After everyone has had a chance to complete the activity, share your own answers. Invite children who want to talk about themselves to share some of their answers also.

Say: "This activity shows us that each of us is unique. God did not make any two people alike. Even people called identical twins are really not identical. You may share some characteristics with others and may look a lot like some of your family members, but there is not another you. You are God's creation. You are God's masterpiece."

3. GOD-PEOPLE FRIENDSHIPS (Workbook page 6)

Guide the children to turn in their workbooks to page 6 Say: "God made us so that we could have a friendship with him. The message of the whole Bible is that God's plan was for people to know him and be a part of our lives. In the Bible there are many people who had great friendships with God. Let's look up the scriptures on the right hand side of the page and discover who it is talking about." With older children, have them work this page independently and then discuss each match. With younger children you may want to look up the Scripture together and work as a group.

4. THE WORLD'S BIG LIE (Workbook page 4)

Say: Can you tell me what the Big Truth for today is? ('God created me to be his friend.') If everyone in the world believed this wonderful truth, we would not even have to teach this lesson today. Unfortunately, most people in our world believe just the opposite. The World's Big Lie is 'I don't need God's friendship.' Some people feel that it is fine to go to church and learn about God, but they do not want a close friendship with him. God wants to be at the center of our lives because he loves us, and he knows what is best for us and what will truly make us happy."

5. THINKING ABOUT BEING FRIENDS (Workbook page 7)

Have the children work in pairs as they think through possible answers to the

questions. After the pairs have had some time to come up with answers, review this page as a group.

Question 1. What do you do to get to know your friends better? (Spend time together, talk, do things together, share your experiences and stories with each other.)

Question 2. How can you be a friend with God when you can't even see him? (Get to know God through prayer and Bible reading.)

Question 3. How is being friends with God different from being friends with a person? (God is always with us; we don't need a telephone to talk to him. Point out to the children that our friendship with God is not a friendship of equals.)

Question 4. Tell of a time you felt close to God. (Leaders need to share their personal experiences first to help children understand this concept.)

6. WAYS I CAN ENJOY A FRIENDSHIP WITH GOD

(Workbook page 8)

Say: "Most of us in this group agree that we believe the Big Truth for today. But it is not enough just to say we agree God is our friend. We need to show by our actions that we believe God created us to be his friend."

Ask children to complete the worksheet. The answers to this worksheet are underlined below.

- _Talk_ to God in prayer.
- _Trust_ God to care for me.
- _Read_ my Bible to learn about God.
- _Worship_ God with all my heart.
- _Obey_ God's commands.
- _Go to church_ and join others in Bible study and worship.

7. MEMORIZE EXODUS 34:14

Say: "Children, I want to conclude today's session with this Bible verse." Let the children follow along as you read Exodus 34:14: "You must worship no other gods, but only the LORD, for he is a God who is passionate about his relationship with you."

Say: "When we are passionate about something that means that we care so much about it that we put all our energy and thought into it. We often say people are passionate about sports or reading or other things that take the very best of their time and energy. The Bible says that God's big passion is knowing you and having you get to know him! This would be a great verse to memorize." Give each child the copy of the memory verse from the memory verse cards in the back of their workbooks. Spend a few minutes helping the children commit this verse to memory. Ask them to take the card home and memorize it during the week, so they can recite it as they enter the classroom the next week. Challenge older students to memorize the whole verse, while younger children can only memorize a shortened version.

8. PRAY

Thank God for being passionate about having a friendship with people. Ask God to give your children a passion to get to know him better.

True or False

Session 1	Session 2	Session 3	Session 4
God created me to be his friend. Stand up and clasp hands together, like a hand shake.	**God is holy and takes my sin seriously.** Use arms and hands to make an X across the face.		

Session 5	Session 6	Session 7	Session 8

SESSION 2
WHAT SIN DOES TO MY FRIENDSHIP WITH GOD

SESSION GOALS

As a result of this session, children should be able to:

- Understand that a Holy God cannot be part of sin.
- Admit that sin has destroyed their friendship with God.
- Identify that sin always has negative consequences.
- Memorize Scripture that teaches that all people sin.

TODAY'S BIG TRUTH: God is holy and takes my sin seriously.

THE WORLD'S BIG LIE: I can decide what is right or wrong for me.

KEY SCRIPTURES FOR TODAY'S SESSION

Genesis 2:8–9, 15–17; 6:11–13; Habakkuk 1:13; Luke 15:11–13; Romans 8:19–21

MEMORY VERSE: Romans 3:12

Older Children "All have turned away from God; all have gone wrong. No one does good, not even one."

Younger Children "All have turned away from God; all have gone wrong."

True or False

LEADERS NEED TO KNOW

The Good News is that a holy God wants to be our friend! The sad truth is sin has broken our friendship with God. Sin is choosing our selfish way against God. We have all sinned, and the result of our sin is separation from God. Today's Big Truth is, ***God is holy and takes my sin seriously.*** It is human nature to deny or excuse our failure, and children have difficulty admitting they are wrong. Some older children reason that if they do something wrong, it doesn't really matter because God will forgive. Grace and forgiveness are truly at the heart of God's plan, but there is a reason we need to be forgiven—sin destroys our friendship with God.

Today we will confront the World's Big Lie that ***"I can decide what is right or wrong for me."*** The common thought even among our children is that what is right or wrong really depends on the situation or on personal preferences. Children must be taught that God has a standard for our behavior, and he has placed his standards for our moral behavior in the Bible. When we choose to adjust God's laws to fit our selfish desires, we sin.

Another misconception children often have about sin is that there are big sins and little sins. Obviously, there are some sins that certainly have more serious consequences here on earth. In relationship to God, however, there are no levels of disobedience. All sin is a big deal to God. A future session will deal with forgiveness of sin, but before people can be forgiven, they must understand that they are sinners.

A caution must be raised concerning the teaching of this session. As a Christian children's worker, you are an instrument in the hands of God, but you are not the Holy Spirit. Only the Holy Spirit can convict and convince a child that he or she has sinned against God. You can provide information and point out what the Bible teaches about sin. But be careful not to talk about sin in such a way that elicits an unhealthy sense of guilt or self-condemnation. At the same time, you must be a believer in the miracle of salvation, and know that it is possible for some of the children whom you teach to be ready to accept Christ as their Lord and Savior.

GEAR UP FOR THE TRUTH

(10 MINUTES)

PREPARE
❑ Stickers
❑ Bubble wrap cut into 6" squares

PROVIDE
❑ Dice
❑ Bubble wrap cut into 6" squares; one for each student and teacher

1. MEMORY VERSE

Allow children to recite last week's memory verse if they memorized it. Give stickers to those who made a serious attempt.

2. DON'T POP THE BUBBLE WRAP

After the children say their memory verses, give them a square of bubble wrap. Ask them not to pop any of the bubbles until they are told to do so. Send them to talk with another adult leader until it is time to start the game. All adult leaders should be prepared to interact personally with the children as they arrive at their tables. Begin by reviewing conversationally the content from session one. The whole time they should be watching to see that the bubbles are not popped. Assign the children to the leaders so that each leader has the same number of children. They do not have to be in their permanent small groups for this introductory game. Make the rules very clear.

Say: "A person from each group will come to me and roll a die. Then each member of the group can pop that many bubbles. Then the representative from the next group gets to roll the die and each member of the group can pop that many bubbles. The first group to pop all their bubbles wins!" Once the popping has begun, some children might start popping bubbles out of turn. Remind them of the rules. If they haven't started to pop the bubbles after moving once or twice around, adult leaders should start breaking the rules.

Say: "It's really hard to sit here and not pop these bubbles! I really wish it were my turn. Whoops! Did you hear something?" As leaders start popping, kids will follow. Laugh with the children as they pop away. Gain control of the group and move the class to the area of the room where you will have your large-group time. Be sure to take up the used bubble wrap.

TEACH THE TRUTH

(25 MINUTES)

PREPARE

❑ Dramatic Skit (see activity 3)

PROVIDE

❑ Bibles

❑ Dry-erase board or chalk board

❑ Dry-erase markers

1. PREPARE AND REVIEW

To help children focus on the session, regain the group's composure by singing a song or two that is familiar and a favorite of the group.

Say: "You all had a lot of fun bursting those bubbles. I'd like for us to stop and think seriously now about what happened." **Ask:** "What were the rules of the game? How did we break them? Was there anyone who didn't break the rules?" **Say:** "Once you got your bubble wrap in your hands, it was probably a strong temptation to burst them. Most kids like to pop bubbles." Continue to explain that the point of this game is that even though we were clearly given the rules of the game, we were all tempted to break the rules and most of us broke the rules.

Ask: "What was the Big Truth we discovered last week? What was the World's Big Lie?" Listen to their responses. **Say:** "Last week we learned that God created us for friendship with himself. Knowing this should make us feel we are important to God. It should also make us want to get to know him and develop our friendship with him. Today we are going to learn what keeps us from knowing and loving God the way that God planned."

2. STUDY THE BIBLE—Genesis 2:8-9;15-17

Guide the children to open their Bibles to Genesis 2. Read Genesis 2:8-9, 15-17: "Then the LORD God planted a garden in Eden, in the east, and there he placed the man he had created. And the Lord God planted all sorts of trees in the garden–beautiful trees that produced delicious fruit. At the center of the garden he placed the tree of life and the tree of the knowledge of good and evil. The Lord God placed the man in the Garden of Eden to tend and care for it. But the Lord God gave him this warning: "You may freely eat any fruit in

the garden except fruit from the tree of the knowledge of good and evil. If you eat of its fruit, you will surely die."

Ask:
- Did God give Adam and Eve a rule to live by?
  (*yes*)

- What was God's clearly given rule?
  (*Adam and Eve were not to eat of the tree of the knowledge of good and evil.*)

- Why did God give them this rule?
  (*God wanted to give Adam and Eve an opportunity to obey him to show their love for him. If they did not have any rules, they would not have the ability to make any choices for themselves. They would have been like puppets and not people who could make the choice to please God.*)

- Could have Adam and Eve made the choice to obey God?
  (*Yes, it was possible.*)

3. DRAMATIC SKIT

Before class, have two adults prepare the following skit. Both actors should be hidden from view behind a curtain or partition. Their voices should be dramatic, clear, and audible. You may serve as the narrator. The Scripture used is from Genesis 3, loosely taken from the New Living Translation (NLT) of the Bible.

Say: "Children, listen carefully as you hear the voices of Eve, the first woman God made, and the serpent in the Garden of Eden. As you listen, discover what keeps people from having a friendship with God."

Narrator: Now the serpent was the shrewdest of all creatures the Lord God had made.

Serpent: Eve, did God really say you must not eat any of the fruit in the garden?

Eve: Of course we may eat it. It's only the fruit from the tree at the center of the garden that we are not allowed to eat. God says we must not eat it or even touch it, or we will die.

Serpent: You won't die! God knows that your eyes will be opened when you eat it. You will become just like God, knowing everything, both good and evil.

Eve: Hmm, the fruit looks so fresh and delicious, and it would make me so wise! I sure want to be wise. That works for me! Adam, try this fruit! It's great!

Ask: "Why did Adam and Eve choose to eat the forbidden fruit?" The children may answer because it looked good and tasty, or that it would make them wise. Help the children discover that when Adam and Eve chose to eat the fruit, they showed they wanted to live to please themselves and not God. They chose to believe one of the world's oldest Big Lies: **"I can decide what is right or wrong for me."** That is what sin is–choosing our own self-ish way and not choosing God's way which is always right.

Say: "I hope that Adam and Eve were able to enjoy the perfect Garden of Eden for a while before they sinned, but the Bible teaches us that one sad day they chose to eat the fruit from the forbidden tree. They sinned, and life on earth is no longer what God origi-nally planned for it to be. Sin is choosing to do things our own way instead of God's way. When we choose to decide for our-selves what is right and wrong, it will always result in what is not best for us."

4. SIN CHANGED EVERYTHING

Say: "The Bible teaches us that through Adam and Eve's disobedience sin entered the world. This was the first act of disobedience to God. Unfortunately, it was not the last act of disobedience to God."

Read aloud Genesis 6:5–7: "Now the Lord observed the extent of the people's wickedness, and he saw that all their thoughts were consis-tently and totally evil. So the Lord was sorry he had ever made them. It broke his heart. And the Lord said, 'I will completely wipe out this

human race that I have created. Yes, and I will destroy all the animals and birds too. I am sorry I ever made them.'"

Say: "What does the Bible say people were like? (*Wicked and evil.*) How did it make God feel? (*It broke his heart.*) Why did God feel sad? (*Because evil and sin had destroyed his friendship with his creation.*)

Read aloud Romans 8:19–21: "For all creation is waiting eagerly for that future day when God will reveal who his children really are. Against its will, everything on earth was subjected to God's curse. All creation anticipates the day when it will join God's children in glorious freedom from death and decay."

Say: "Sin hurts our friendship with God. The only way we can be friends again with God is if he provides for the forgiveness of our sin. We will learn more in the next few weeks about how Jesus' death on the cross is God's solution to our separation from God and his friendship."

5. TODAY'S BIG TRUTH
Say: "The Big Truth for today is: **God is Holy and takes my sin seriously.**" Teach the children the actions for this Big Truth. Guide them to repeat this truth and actions with you. In the center of a white marker board, write the word HOLY. Ask the children to brainstorm with you what they think the word holy means. (Record possible answers: morally perfect, pure, set apart for God, sacred.)

Say: "Our Big Truth states that God is holy, which means he never does wrong. But when we choose to do wrong things, we turn away from him. That breaks God's heart, because he wants our friendship. That's why our sin is such a big deal to God."

6. THE WORLD'S BIG LIE
Say: "The world around us has another big lie for us to believe. Many people believe that we can each decide for ourselves what is right and wrong. The world would have me believe that I can decide what is right or wrong for me. Think about you and your friends and some examples of how kids your age decided for themselves what was right or wrong. How could thinking like this be danger-

ous?" Listen to their examples, and talk through them with the children.

Optional idea: *Read The Topsy Turvy Kingdom* by Josh McDowell.

7. INTRODUCE THE PARABLE OF THE LOST SON

Say: "In the Bible, Jesus told a story about a young man who believed that he could decide for himself what was right or wrong. In the weeks to come we are going to cover this whole story, but today we are just going to read the section about the choice the young man made based on his wrong thinking. Open your Bibles to Luke 15:11–13." When the children have found the scripture, read:

"To illustrate the point further, Jesus told them this story: 'A man had two sons. The younger son told his father, 'I want my share of your estate now, instead of waiting until you die.' So his father agreed to divide his wealth between his sons. A few days later this younger son packed all his belongings and took a trip to a distant land, and there he wasted all his money on wild living."

Say: "What did the younger son want?" (*He wanted his inheritance even before his father had died.*) You may have to explain to the children what an inheritance or "my share of the estate" is. Younger children will usually have no idea that they will receive what their parents leave behind. Discuss with the children what was wrong with the son's thinking. Point out the following:

• The son wanted his father's money even before his father had died.
• The son wanted to live away from his father.
• The son ran away from the father to live the way he wanted and do wrong things.

During the next six weeks you will hear more of this story. It finally has a happy ending. And I can hardly wait to share the whole story with you!"

Say: "We are all like that son in this story. We have all run away from God, our Father. We've run away from God, our greatest friend. Romans 3:12 says, 'All have turned away from God; all have gone wrong. No one does good, not even one.' This is our biggest problem. But God loved us so much, that he provided a plan so we could be forgiven. We need God's love and forgiveness. This verse, Romans 3:12, is our memory verse this week. Let's each

quietly study it for a minute or two and then I'll call on volunteers to say this verse aloud. This is a good verse to know because it reminds us that we need to ask for God's forgiveness for our sin."

8. PRAY
Ask God to help you understand that he wants to be your friend, but your sin has broken that friendship.

APPLY THE TRUTH TO LIFE
(25 MINUTES–SMALL-GROUP TIME)

PROVIDE
❏ *True or False* children's workbooks
❏ Pens / pencils

1. GREET AND REVIEW
Welcome the children back to your table and briefly review the day's theme. Say: "In our large-group time today, we learned about a son who took his dad's money and ran away from home. When we sin, we behave just like that lost son. We run away from God."

Ask: "How do you think God feels when we do wrong?" (*sad; his heart is broken*).
Say: "You are right; our sin hurts God. That is what we are going to learn more about in our time together."

2. DISCUSS GOD'S ATTITUDE TOWARD SIN
God is totally pure. Find and read Habakkuk 1:13: "Your eyes are too pure to look on evil; you cannot tolerate wrong."

God wants to be friends with each of us, but our sins separate us from God. The wrong things we do break God's laws, and they hurt other people God cares about. Since God only does what is right and loving and perfect, he must do something about sin. In order for us to be a close friend with God, he provided the answer to our problem of sin. That's why he sent Jesus to earth so that he could make a way for God to forgive us of our sins.

3. AS A RESULT OF SIN . . . (Workbook page 10)
Have the children turn to page 10 in their workbooks and discover the results of sin. Carefully discuss the content of this workbook activity. Older children can

work independently on this workbook activity. You may want to do this page as a group project for younger children.

Say: "Sin came into the world through the very first couple, Adam and Eve. Adam and Eve lived in a beautiful garden where all their needs were met. It would be nice to end this story with 'and they lived happily ever after.' Actually this was God's plan for them. But their sin changed everything."

The answers to the activity:
1. A **CURSE** was placed on the **GROUND**. The land would grow **THORNS** and **THISTLES**. (Genesis 3:17–18)
2. Adam would have to **STRUGGLE** to make a **LIVING**. (Genesis 3:17)
3. Though Eve would still have children, and childbearing would still bring her joy, it would also bring intense **PAIN**. (Genesis 3:16)
4. The serpent would grovel in the **DUST** and **CRAWL** on his **BELLY**. (Genesis 3:14)
5. God **BANISHED** them from the garden. (Genesis 3:23)

[Activity #4 does not appear in the younger book.]

4. CREATE A VISUAL REMINDER

Give each child a clean sheet of white paper. Ask them to describe the sheet (*pure, white, neat, clean*). Next ask them to crumple their paper into a tight ball. If they want to do so, they can they can cut or tear their paper. Then ask them to smooth out their paper and present it on the table in front of them. Then lay a new clean sheet of paper in the middle and ask them to compare their paper to the clean new sheet of paper. Discuss the differences.

Say: " You were allowed to have your own way with that sheet of paper. That is exactly what happens when we try to have our own way in our lives apart from God. Having our own way and disobeying God makes God sad because it hurts our friendship with him."

5. I CAN CHOOSE TO AGREE WITH GOD (Workbook page 11)

Say: "Today's Big Truth is *God is holy and takes sin seriously,* and there's also a Big Lie we need to watch out for: 'I can decide what is right and wrong for me.' That's a huge lie."

Ask:
- What did you learn today that tells you that sin hurts our friendship with God?"
- What sorts of things cause us to run away from God?
- If you really believe that sin hurts your friendship with God, how would you choose to act?

Have older students match the verses to the statements, then give an example of a choice they've faced and how one of the scriptures can help them. (Answers: Decide to follow God–Prov. 4:23); Know and act on God's commands–Ps. 119:11; Pick friends who will help–2 Tim. 2:22)

Discuss temptations with younger students then ask them to draw a picture of them making a right choice.

6. HELP WANTED (Workbook page 12)

Say: "Kids, the truth is, the way we behave shows God and others what we truly believe. There are four problems people face when it comes to deciding about what is right or wrong:
- Have difficulty admitting they have sinned.

- Misunderstand God's forgiveness.

- Rate sins as little or big.

- Excuse their sin.

Say: "Each of the four children in this activity has one of these problems. How can you help them?" Read the scenarios aloud to the children. Then discuss the solutions as a group.

7. PRAY

Ask God to make you more aware of how your behavior affects your friendship with him.

True or False

Session 1	Session 2	Session 3	Session 4
God created me to be his friend.	**God is holy and takes my sin seriously.**	**Sin separates me from God.**	
Stand up and clasp hands together, like a hand shake.	Use arms and hands to make an X across the face.	With arms extended forward in front of their body, hands flexed with fingers pointed upward, take two steps back..	

Session 5	Session 6	Session 7	Session 8

SESSION 3
LOST AND ALONE BECAUSE OF SIN

SESSION GOALS:
As a result of this session, children should be able to:
- State that the result of sin is separation from God.
- Understand that sin makes people feel guilty as well as lost and alone.
- Identify the difference between sin and sins.
- Memorize Scripture that teaches the result of sin is spiritual death.
- Believe that without God's help there is no escape from sin.

TODAY'S BIG TRUTH: Sin separates me from God.

THE WORLD'S BIG LIE: I can live my life my way.

KEY SCRIPTURES FOR TODAY'S SESSION: Luke 15:13–15

MEMORY VERSES:

Older Children
Romans 3:23 "For all have sinned; all fall short of God's glorious standard."
Romans 6:23 "For the wages of sin is death, but the free gift of God is eternal life through Christ Jesus our Lord."

Younger Children
Romans 3:23 "For all have sinned; all fall short of God's glorious standard."
Romans 6:23 "the free gift of God is eternal life through Christ Jesus our Lord."

True or False

LEADERS NEED TO KNOW

The goal in this session is to take the information about sin and make it personal. Children need to know that sin makes a person feel separated from God. Many people call this feeling being lost or alone from God. Impress on the children that something very important is missing in our lives when we are not living in fellowship with God.

Be honest with children. Sin can be appealing. If it were not, we would not be tempted to sin! Sin can be convenient. Children often lie because it is the easy way out. In fact sometimes sin can seem to be "friendly." We can reason that to refuse to go along with the group will make others feel uncomfortable or cause us to be an outsider.

We can find so many ways to excuse and justify our sin. This is true because of the World's Big Lie we are going to expose today: *"I can live my life my way."* Help the children discover that a willful selfishness deep in our heart makes us want to do things our way–even when we know it is not the best way. This attitude of selfishness is resistance toward God, which is exactly what sin is. Some of the half-truths we tell ourselves include:
  • I will not get caught.
  • I'm not that bad.
  • I know people who sin more than me.
  • God will forgive me anyway.

One result of sin is guilt. Children are sensitive and are easily made to feel guilty. So be careful not to teach this session in such a way that you induce guilt. Help children realize that guilt is an emotion. There is real guilt, and false guilt. When we have truly done something wrong, we must admit it and do whatever we can to make that situation right. Help children get to the place where they
  • admit they sin;
  • agree with God that sin hurts them and their friendship with him;
  • look for ways to resist temptation to sin when it comes their way.

GEAR UP FOR THE TRUTH
(10 MINUTES)

PREPARE
❑ Using bright colored paper, place them all over the floor of the room.

❑ Name tags for all the adult teachers saying "Official Inspector."

PROVIDE
❑ Stickers

❑ Large floor area. An adjacent unused room where you can move the furniture out or against the wall would work the best. You may want to get creative and place some furniture in spaces that would make this activity more difficult if you have older children.

❑ Bright colored 8 1/2 x 11 sheets of paper, as many as 50 sheets depending on the space you have and the amount of children doing this activity.

❑ Pictures of extravagant, exaggerated prizes (that are not actual), such as a trip to Hawaii or a jet ski.

1. MEMORY VERSE
Allow children to recite last week's memory verse, and give a sticker to those who seriously make an effort.

2. DON'T FALL INTO SIN!
Explain to the children that they are to cross the length of the room as many times as they can, stepping only on the bright colored pieces of paper and never touching the floor. Each time they cross the room and return, they will receive a point. Each time they "fall into sin" (touch the floor) they will lose a point. All the children may end up with a negative account. That would be good and help make our point. You can really make this exciting by telling them they can turn in their points for a particular prize. Have coveted prizes present. However make the activity so challenging that no one can win anything! Yes, we want this to be frustrating.

The teachers will have to be diligent to keep score. Expect some complaints, just tell the kids to try harder! Cheer them on. **Say:** "I know you can do it" This activity will provide some good physical exercise.

TEACH THE TRUTH

(25 MINUTES)

PREPARE

❑ Write the Romans 3:23 passage on a marker board.

❑ Visual aid posters:

• Poster 1: On a poster, write "SINS–The things we say, do, or think which the Bible tells us are wrong and are against God's will."

• Poster 2: On a poster, write "SIN – Choosing our own selfish way to live and not choosing to obey God's plan for us."

• Poster 3: Write, "Because we have a SIN nature we commit many SINS."

PROVIDE

❑ Marker board; dry-erase markers

1. DISCUSS THE "DON'T FALL INTO SIN" ACTIVITY

Say: "I am so sorry no one was able to win any of these fabulous prizes!"

Ask: "So how did you feel about the game?" They should complain about how impossible it was. Conclude the discussion by saying that you know it was frustrating and impossible. Tell them that's why you called it "Don't Fall into Sin." **Say:** "As much as we may have tried in our own efforts, it was impossible not to fall into sin. Sin has kept us from reaching the prize or goal that God has for us."

2. STUDY THE BIBLE—ROMANS 3:23

Say: "We all fall short of God's perfect goal. Pretty frustrating goal? Very! Impossible? Yes!"

Call attention to the white marker board on which you have written today's memory verse. This is a short verse and one many children may have already memorized.

Ask: "Whom does this verse say has sinned?" (*everyone*). **Say** (with an incredulous look on your face): "You mean that I have sinned?" Most older children will be glad to say, "Yes!" A few may be too polite to say it. Some younger children may not yet see teachers

as sinners. Explain what "fall short" means. Equate it to running a race. Someone wins, the others fall short of the goal. Be sure that children are able to state the goal God has for our lives–that sin no longer separates us from him. Point to the unclaimed prizes, and tell the children that they aren't nearly as valuable as the prize God has for us: eternal life with him in heaven.

Read the verse on the dry-erase board together. Erase a word and have them say it again, filling in the blanks. Erase two words and have them read the verse again. Continue until all that is left is "Romans 3:23." Ask if any child would like to say the verse alone. Clean off the board and allow volunteers to take turns quoting Romans 3:23.

3. SPEAKING ABOUT FEELINGS ...

Write the word SIN in the center of the white marker board. **Ask:** "When you do something that you know is wrong, something that God calls sin, how does it make you feel?" Write the answers the children provide around the word sin on the white marker board (*guilty, bad, sad, fearful, etc*). If children do not say "lost" and "alone" provide those answers and help them understand that sin makes us feel away from God and alone.

Say: "Wow, this is a bunch of bad stuff. I am so glad that God cares about the way we feel. I am so thankful that God is willing to provide us with a way to reach the goal and win that prize. I am looking forward to telling you about how Jesus' death on the cross is the answer to the problem that we have with sin."

4. BACK TO THE STORY OF THE LOST SON

Briefly review the story of the lost son that has already been covered in the previous session. Ask the children to find Luke 15:13–15 in their Bibles. **Say:** "Listen to what happens next." Then read the passage and discuss the story.

"A few days later this younger son packed all his belongings and took a trip to a distant land, and there he wasted all his money on wild living. About the time his money ran out, a great famine swept over the land, and he began to starve. He persuaded a local farmer to hire him to feed his pigs. The boy became so hungry that even the pods he was feeding the pigs looked good to him. But no one gave him anything."

Ask: "What did the son do when he went away from home? (*He wasted all his money on wild living.*) What happened in the far distant land where he went to live? (*A great famine swept over the land.*) How did the famine affect the son? (*He began to starve.*) So what did the boy do? (*He got a job feeding pigs.*) How did the son feel about what he was doing? (*He was so hungry that the pigs' food looked good to him.*)

Be sure and interject that there is nothing wrong with feeding pigs. **Say:** Many people in our country feed pigs every day so we can have ham and bacon. Pig farms in our country are carefully regulated so that they are clean. But in Bible times, pigs were considered dirty. God had even given his people a law against eating pork or working with pigs. So what this story is telling us, is that the son got the very worst kind of work possible for a Jewish man to have."

Say: "The last sentence in this Bible story says, 'But no one gave him anything.' The lost son was truly alone. He must have felt lonely and sad. He was totally separated from the person who could help him most--his father. Sin separates us from God, just like the son in our story is separated from his father. This separation from God leaves us feeling alone."

5. DRAMATIZE SEPARATION FROM GOD

Act out what it means for us to be separated from God. Have one of the adults stand in the middle of the room wearing a sign that says "God." Ask the children to bunch around him or her in a group hug. **Ask:** "How close are we now?" Have everyone, except the adult wearing the sign that says "God" take one step back.

Say: "That's what happens to us when we sin. Step back again. Each time we sin we are further and further from God. Take another step back. Now none of us can reach God. Take another step back. Now we can't even reach each other." Keep taking one step back until no one can stretch a hand out to "God" or anyone else.

Maintain quiet, and ask children to sit wherever they are in the room. Remind them that they are out of touch with everyone else in the room. Emphasize the seriousness of being totally alone and unable to find our way back to God. **Say:** "The wrong things we do take us so far away that we are totally alone and can't find our way back to God."

Say: "The Bible calls that painful kind of separation 'death.' When somebody dies, we're completely cut off from that person. That's physical death. But there's another kind of death that is even worse. 'Spiritual death' is when people are separated far from God. Our

memory verse, Romans 6:23, says 'For the wages of sin is death, but the free gift of God is eternal life through Christ Jesus our Lord.' When people sin they earn what sin pays–death. That sounds bad, but this verse also has good news in it: 'but the free gift of God is eternal life through Christ Jesus our Lord.' I hope that when you come back next week you can recite this verse to me."

6. SIN AND SINS—BRAINSTORM

Say: "Many people will admit that they are not perfect, but they really do not think that anything they have done was bad enough for Jesus to have to die on the cross for them."

Write the word **SINS** in the center of a marker board. **Ask**: "What are some examples of things that children your age do that are wrong? Write their answers on the white marker board so that all the sins mentioned are displayed. **Ask**: "Which of the words on this board are things that the Bible teaches us will displease God?" Call for a volunteer to circle the words that the Bible says are sins. Most of the words will be circled. Erase any words that have not been circled.

Say: "We have agreed that all these things are wrong, and all these things are considered sins in the Bible. Do you think that anything on this list is so bad that Jesus would have to die on the cross?" **Say:** "These are all **sins**." Call attention to the visual aid, Poster 1, you made on sins before class, which defines sins as "the things we say, do, or think which the Bible tells us are wrong and are against God's will."

Next demonstrate the visual aid, Poster 2, on sin (without the "s"). **Say:** "Sin is choosing our own selfish way to live and not choosing to obey God's plan for us." While demonstrating the two visual aids, help the children see the difference, which is that all people have a problem with sin. Then show visual aid, Poster 3. **Say:** That is why Jesus died on the cross, because we have gone against God's will for our lives. Because we have a sin nature, we commit many sins. (Sometimes the concept is tough even for adults to follow, but present it to the children, and be as clear as possible.)

7. PRAY

Ask the children to bow their heads and close their eyes and lead them in prayer. Ask God to help each one understand how sin affects their friendship with him. Thank and praise God for not leaving us alone. Thank God that he wants to remove our aloneness and be our close friend.

8. WRAP-UP THIS LARGE-GROUP TIME

Say: "I know we left the lost son in the pig pen, but it is not the end of his story. I know you want to hear the rest of the story, and I'm going to enjoy telling it to you." Dismiss to small groups.

APPLY THE TRUTH TO LIFE

(25 MINUTE–SMALL-GROUP TIME)

PROVIDE
❑ *True or False* children's workbooks

1. GREET AND REVIEW

The content of the large-group time was pretty heavy, so lighten up with the kids and give them a few minutes to connect to you and the others in the group on a personal level. Pull out the chart of the Big Truths that we are learning and review the two Big Truths and motions you have taught thus far.

Say: "Let's read all eight Big Truths we will study in this series so you can see that we are going to keep on learning about God's plan." Have the children practice all the Big Truths. They can find all eight on the last page of their workbook. The Big Truths are found in this Leaders Guide on pages 22, 38 and 116.

2. TODAY'S BIG TRUTH

Say: "The Big Truth for today is **Sin separates me from God.**" Have the children look at the chart and duplicate the motion: extend both arms forward, palms out, with fingers pointing upward, and take two steps back (as if pushing away).

Say: "During our large-group time you learned that sin means we are separated from God. No one else can rescue us. Your parents love you very much and there is probably nothing they would want to do for you more than to rescue you from your sin and make sure that you go to heaven. But even your parents cannot help you here. Your pastor or friends, or teachers have no power to rescue you. And there is nothing you alone can do either. Only God can provide a way. God has a plan to rescue us. He wants to forgive us of our sin that separates us from him, so we will no longer be alone. God says there is a penalty that must be paid for sin, which is death. The good news is that God sent his Son, Jesus

to pay that penalty for our sin. Jesus died for us so that God could forgive us of sin and become our dear friend."

3. DISCUSS THE WORLD'S BIG LIE

Say: "The world has a Big Lie that some people believe: *'I can live my life my way.'* The truth is, we all want our own way.

Say: "How can thinking this way be dangerous to us?" (*It will keep us separated from God; it can even ruin our relationships with others; it produces feelings of guilt.*)

4. THE TRUTH ABOUT SIN (Workbook page 16)

Guide children to work through this workbook page. Older children should be able to complete this individually. With younger children you may want to do it as a group.

The answers and Scripture to back them up are listed below.

1. An action isn't a sin if you don't feel bad when you do it. FALSE. Your conscience often tells you the difference between right and wrong, but sin is really about breaking God's commands. Romans 3:23 says that to sin is to "fall short of God's glorious standard."

2. There are some really good people like grandparents and pastors who have never committed a sin. FALSE. Romans 3:23 also says, "All have sinned."

3. Little sins like "white lies" are not a big deal to God. FALSE. James 2:10 says, "The person who keeps all of the laws except one is as guilty as the person who has broken all of God's laws"

4. I'm not so bad; lots of people are bigger sinners than I am. FALSE. The Bible compares each of us to God–not to each other. Romans 3:12 says "All have turned away from God; all have gone wrong. No one does good, not even one."

5. If I can do a lot of good things, I can make up for the bad things I do. FALSE. Ephesians 2:9 says, "Salvation is not a reward for the good things we have done, so none of us can boast about it."

5. CHOOSE TO OBEY GOD'S WAYS—CROSSWORD PUZZLE
(Workbook page 17)

Older children will enjoy working a crossword puzzle that will provide reminders of the kinds of behavior God expects of them.

1. Tell the truth; do not _____. (lie)
2. Pay for what you take from a store, do not _____. (steal)
3. Control your _____ when you get angry. (temper)
4. Treat other kids with respect. Do not kick or _____ them. (hit)
5. Obey your parents and do not _____ them. (disrespect)
6. Speak kindly of others, do not _____. (gossip)
7. Study hard so that you will not be tempted to _____ in school. (cheat)
8. Avoid _____ that displease God because he cares about what you see. (movies)
9. Learn to tell clean jokes and not _____ ones. (dirty)
10. Respect your body and do not do _____. (drugs)

The younger children's simpler activity requires that they put an X on the picture of children who are making a wrong choice. After they've had time to work, go over the pictures together.

6. ESCAPE! (Workbook page 18)

Say: "Well, it seems like we have learned about a lot of things that are wrong to do. The big question now is, when faced with temptation, what do we do? The answer is ESCAPE! There is a Bible verse that tells us God will always provide us with a way to escape temptation!"

Read 1 Corinthians 10:13:
'But remember that the temptations that come into your life are no different from what others experience. And God is faithful. He will keep the temptation from becoming so strong that you can't stand up against it. When you are tempted, he will show you a way out so that you will not give in to it.'

The very next time you are tempted to do something wrong, ask God to help you escape it–to show you a way out–just like this verse promises he will do. Let's practice how to escape temptations. Turn in your workbooks to page 18."

Read the verse at the top of the page.

Say: "Can you help Randy, Kim, and Carlos think of a way they can escape their temptation? All three of these kids go to church and will tell you they love Jesus, but they are each tempted to do what they know they should not do." Read the three scenarios and discuss how each can escape temptation.

A. Randy has great friends at church, but only one of them is in his class at school. He is very outgoing and likes to be in the "in" crowd. The one boy in his class at both school and church is not really in with the cool kids. When Randy is with his church friends, he does okay, but he is unsure of himself with his school friends. He really wants to impress his school friends with how cool he is. The guys in the group he runs with often tell jokes that make him feel uncomfortable. He knows that the words they are saying displease God and would not please his parents. But he really wants to hang around and hear the jokes. He is so afraid of what the other guys would think if they knew how he felt, so he tries to laugh and play along. It is just so tempting to join in.

What is Randy's way of escape?

_____

_____

_____

_____.

B. Kim is smart and can make good grades. She really likes to study and wants to always make A's. She becomes so upset if she gets a B. One day, while helping her teacher out, she found where the teacher kept the test that she was planning to give on Friday. Kim slipped a copy of the test out quickly, and she was able to study with it. When she took the test in class, it was very easy for her because she had already worked it out. When she got a perfect score and then got by with it, she was thrilled. Unfortunately, she has developed a habit of snooping around the teacher's desk and watching carefully where the teacher puts things. Taking another test almost seems like a game. It would be so tempting.

What is Kim's way of escape?

_____

_____

_____

_____ .

C. Carlos really loves his parents very much but he thinks they have too many rules for him. His parents pay for his school lunches ahead of time so that he will not have to carry money to school each day. They have also explained that this way they can be sure that he gets the whole meal of the day, and is not spending his lunch money in the vending machines full of soft drinks and junk food. Deep down inside Carlos knows his parents are doing the right thing, but he wants the stuff some of his friends are eat–ing. He has thought of talking to his parents about his feelings, but then he discovered a large jar, where his parents drop change, in their bedroom closet. Carlos is careful to not get caught but for the last two weeks, almost daily he has been able to buy something from the vending machines. He knows he should stop this behavior, but it is just too tempting.

What is Carlos's way of escape?

_____

_____

_____

_____ .

7. PRAY

Thank God for his love, and ask him to help you find your way of escape whenever you are tempted to sin.

True or False

Session 1	Session 2	Session 3	Session 4
God created me to be his friend.	**God is holy and takes my sin seriously.**	**Sin separates me from God.**	**God sent Jesus to be the Savior of the world.**
Stand up and clasp hands together, like a hand shake.	Use arms and hands to make an X across the face.	With arms extended forward in front of their body, hands flexed with fingers pointed upward, take two steps back..	Touch palm of right hand with the middle finger of left hand, then repeat the gesture with opposite hands, as in the sign language symbol for Jesus, and point to heaven.

Session 5	Session 6	Session 7	Session 8

BELIEF.

SESSION 4
JESUS IS THE ONE AND ONLY SAVIOR

SESSION GOALS:

As a result of this session children will be guided to:

- Acknowledge that Jesus is God the Son.

- Understand that God sent Jesus to be the one and only Savior of the world.

- Feel convinced that there is only one way to come to God, and that way is through Jesus.

- Be able to state that we can recognize Jesus is the Savior through the prophecies about him, the miracles he performed, and his resurrection from the dead.

TODAY'S BIG TRUTH: God sent Jesus to be the Savior of the world.

THE WORLD'S BIG LIE: There are a lot of ways to come to God.

KEY SCRIPTURES FOR TODAY'S SESSION:
Luke 15:17–19; Acts 4:12; 1 John 1:1–2; 4:9

MEMORY VERSE: John 14:6

Older Children

"I am the way, the truth, and the life. No one can come to the Father except through me."

True or False

Younger Children

"Jesus told him, 'I am the way, the truth, and the life.'"

LEADERS NEED TO KNOW

Our children are growing up in a pluralistic culture. Many today in our society are followers of a non-Christian religion. Some may even celebrate Christmas, give gifts and decorate for the holidays–it just doesn't have any religious meaning to them. This is the culture in which our children are growing up. There is a lot of religious talk surrounding our children that has no relationship to Jesus Christ, the one and only God/Man.

As a result, our children will tend to believe that there are a lot of ways to come to God. However, Jesus declares that there is only one way. We want our children to know the Big Truth that **God sent Jesus to be the Savior of the world.**

Here in this lesson we will be exposing the Big Lie that: **"There are a lot of ways to come to God."** Some say that all faiths are right; we are all worshiping the same God–we just have different names for God. Yet those various faiths describe a different and conflicting view of God. We need to help our children become convinced that Jesus' claim to be the Son of the one true God is true, while at the same time teaching our children to be considerate, kind, and respectful toward those who do not believe in Christ. Even young children can develop deepened convictions about who Christ is.

The apostle John provides us an eyewitness account to the fact that Jesus is the only God/man when he said:

"The one who existed from the beginning is the one we have heard and seen. We saw him with our own eyes and touched him with our own hands. He is Jesus Christ, the Word of life. This one who is life from God was shown to us, and we have seen him. And now we testify and announce to you that he is the one who is eternal life." 1 John 1:1–2

Your children will be impressed to discover that hundreds of years before Jesus' birth, many prophecies were made about Jesus which were later fulfilled in his life. Jesus performed miracles that proved he was God, doing things that only God can do. Your children will see that the resurrection of Jesus from the dead was a unique event. Above all, they need to feel loved by Jesus. As you talk about the evidences of Christ being the God/man, remember that "head knowledge" and facts alone will not draw children to him. Express your love for Jesus as you speak, and the children will want to love him, too.

GEAR UP FOR THE TRUTH
(10 MINUTES)

PREPARE

❏ Cutouts of paper dolls or die cuts of children from construction paper (Memory Verse Game #1)

❏ Make the memory verse puzzles as described in Memory Verse Game #2.

❏ On sentence strips write:

> I am the way,
> the truth,
> and the life.
> No one can come
> to the Father
> except through me.
> John 14:6
>   (Memory Verse Game #3)

PROVIDE

❏ Stickers

❏ Optional: Laptop computer for children to type in their memory verses and self–check their accuracy.

❏ Envelopes; paper; construction paper; tag board

❏ Gel pens; fine–tip felt pens

1. MEMORY VERSE GAMES

Give a sticker to arriving students who can type or say last week's memory verse as they arrive. Optional: Award a small prize to those who remember all the memory verses for the previous three weeks.

Assign a teacher to each memory verse game to play with the children.

> **Game #1–Review Exodus 34:14.** If you have access to a die–cut machine and the form of a paper doll or boy and girl figures, precut enough figures for each child to have one. As the children arrive at your table give each child a paper doll figure and have them write out Exodus 34:14 on it with colored pens. Encourage older children to write the verse from memory. Younger children might need to copy a sample or just write the Scripture reference and say the verse aloud.

Game #2–Review Romans 3:12; 3:23; and 6:23. Make individual puzzles of these verses for each child by writing each verse on paper and cutting out each word. Put the puzzle in an envelope labeled with the Scripture reference. As children arrive to your table, have them take an envelope of any of the three Romans verses. Instruct them to take all the words and arrange them in the correct order. When they think they have all the words right, have them call you over to check their work. Ask children to tell you what their verse means. Explain and clarify their thinking concerning their verse. They can then place the verse back in its envelope so another child can put it together. If time remains they can do a second or third verse.

Game #3–Introduce John 14:6. Say: Take time for children to find today's memory verse in their Bibles. Allow a volunteer to read it, or you may read it to younger children. **Say:** "This verse teaches us that there is no other way to come to God except by believing in Jesus." Discuss why the verse calls Jesus "the way, the truth, and the life." Let children close their Bibles, and then arrange the John 14:6 sentence strips you made before class.

2. PRAY
When time is up, get the attention of the children and call them together around you and pray that the children will use the verses they have learned to bring glory to God.

TEACH THE TRUTH
(25 MINUTES)

PREPARE
❑ Visual aid: Poster of "Savior" (Activity 1)
❑ Visual aids: Posters of "Prophecy," "Miracles," and "Resurrection" (See activity 4 for instructions.)
❑ Visual aid: Write the passage for 1 John 1:1–2 on poster board (Activity 3)

PROVIDE
❑ Bibles
❑ Poster board

1. DEFINE "SAVIOR"
Say: "We believe that God sent Jesus into the world as the only one who could solve our problem with sin. You have probably heard Jesus called the Savior." Show the visual aid you made with

"Savior" centered on it. **Ask** the children first to tell you how they would describe the word. Children will say, "Jesus." You want to get them beyond a rote answer to true comprehension of the meaning of *savior*: "one who rescues someone from danger."

Say: "Give me some examples of people who rescue others from danger." The children will think of lifeguards at the swimming pool, or policemen, firemen, doctors and nurses, some may even name parents and teachers. **Ask** the children to tell you how these people save others. **Ask:** "What does Jesus save us from?" Guide children to understand that Jesus wants to save us from separation from God.

2. JESUS IS THE ONE AND ONLY SAVIOR

Say: "The Bible teaches us that Jesus is the one and only Savior. Some people talk about Jesus Christ, but they do not believe that he is the only Son of God and the only way that we can know God and have forgiveness for our sin. That is why it is so important that we understand clearly what we believe about who Jesus is.

We need to be respectful of what others choose to believe. The Bible teaches us that we are to treat everyone kindly no matter what they believe about Jesus. We also must learn all we can about Jesus so that when we are asked questions about what we believe and why we believe that way, we can give people good answers."

Say: "The best way to recognize if something is *True or False* is to know what is true. So for the rest of the time today, we are going to learn how we can know for sure that Jesus is the one and only Savior."

3. STUDY THE BIBLE—1 JOHN 1:1-2

Guide children to find 1 John 1:1 in their Bibles. If you have a volunteer who is a confident reader, allow the child to read the verse to the group. Display the verse on a poster large enough for the whole group to see.

4. HOW WE CAN KNOW JESUS IS THE ONLY SAVIOR

Display your visual aids, each having only one word, "Prophecy," "Miracles," and "Resurrection." As you introduce each one, lay that word on the floor.

Say: "There are three ways we can know that Jesus is the Savior. We can know through:

- **Prophecy**–In the Old Testament–hundreds of years before Jesus was born–God told people that one day a Savior was coming into our world. In your small discussion groups you will discover some of these prophecies and find out how they came true in Jesus' life. There is no way these predictions could all have come true unless Jesus was truly the Son of God.

- **Miracles**–Jesus did things that only God could do! If you have a churched group, ask them to tell the stories of their favorite miracle. If you are leading a group that does not have a strong Bible background, tell them one of your favorite miracle stories and invite the other teachers in the room to share their favorite miracle story also.

- **Resurrection**–**Say:** "On Easter Sunday each year we celebrate Jesus' resurrection. What do I mean when I say we celebrate *resurrection?*" Make sure the children know that after Jesus died on the cross, his disciples buried his body in a tomb, but three days later Jesus came back to life, adding that no one could do that unless he were truly the one-and-only Son of God.

5. LEARN THE MEMORY VERSE—JOHN 14:6

This verse has already been introduced in the introductory activity. Go over it again and see if anyone can say it by memory. After the children have said it a few more times, relate how this verse is proved through prophesies about Jesus, the miracles he did, and his resurrection. Use the sentence strips again with the phrases of the memory verse. Lay out all the sentence strips on the floor and have the children stand in a semicircle facing the verses. Read each strip a few times, helping the children memorize them. Then, remove the strips, one at a time, and have the children recite the whole verse between the removal of each strip. When all the strips have been removed, ask if any children would like to volunteer to quote the whole verse for you. Be careful not to embarrass any children, remembering that children embarrass easier than others. Therefore do not call on any of the children individually to quote the verse; let them volunteer.

6. BACK TO THE STORY OF THE LOST SON

Open your Bible to Luke 15. Remind the children of where we left off with the story last week. Call on a child to tell the story thus far. If there are children present this week who were not here last week, be sure to help them discover what happened to the Lost Son in the previous session. Read aloud verses 17-19 in the New Living Translation, and then discuss the passage:

"When he finally came to his senses, he said to himself, 'At home even the hired men have food enough to spare, and here I am, dying of hunger! I will go home to my father and say, 'Father, I have sinned against both heaven and you, and I am no longer worthy of being called your son. Please take me on as a hired man.'"

Say: "It seems like the lost son started thinking right again. What was he willing to admit to his father?" (*He had sinned against both heaven and his father.*) **Say:** "He did not ask to be taken back as a son. What did he ask his father to do for him?" (*Hire him as a hired hand.*) The best decision he made was to go back to his father for help. We are going to have to wait until next week to find out if his father hired him or not!

7. TODAY'S BIG TRUTH

Say: "The Big Truth for today is ***God sent Jesus to be the Savior of the world.*** But there is also a Big Lie: '***There are a lot of ways to come to God.***' Some people think that people of different religions all worship the same God. You might even hear people say that no matter what names people use for God, they are all talking to the same God. It is true that the word God can be spoken in different languages (for example, the Spanish word for God is Dios). But the questions we need to ask are:

- Did Jesus think there were many ways to come to God?
- How do we know Jesus is who he said he was–the Son of the one and only true God?
- Is believing in Jesus the only way to come to God?
- Should we be unloving toward people because they don't worship Jesus?

Say: "The way we feel about and treat people who do not believe in Jesus is very important. Because God is love, he wants us to act lovingly toward all people."

8. PRAY

Guide your children to thank God that he has given us a way to know that he is the one true God, with whom we can have a close friendship.

APPLY THE TRUTH TO LIFE

(25 MINUTES–SMALL-GROUP TIME)

PROVIDE

❑ *True or False* children's workbooks

❑ Pens / pencils

1. GREET AND REVIEW

Welcome the children who arrive at your table. Take time to review the content that has already been covered today. Ask if any of the children have any questions about what has been said. Many children will be more comfortable asking questions in a small group rather than a large group.

2. ONLY ONE GOD, ONLY ONE SAVIOR (Workbook page 22)

Say: "In your workbook you will discover that the Bible says that Jesus is the only true way to come to God. Jesus taught us that he is the one and only truth." This fill-in-the-blank activity will help the children review lesson-related scriptures.

3. THREE-WAY PROPHECY MATCH (Workbook page 23)

Guide the children to look up the New Testament references and decide which Old Testament prophecies each one fulfilled. The order of the answers is:

Luke 3:23–32; Matthew 2:1; Matthew 9:25; Matthew 26:49; Acts 2:31

Younger children will need you to talk them through each match.

4. REVIEW THE BIG TRUTHS

Go over all four Big Truths studied thus far with the corresponding motions.

5. PRAY

Close your time by thanking God that he has given us so much proof that he is the one true way to God, so we would not miss out on having a friendship with him. Focus this prayer on how passionate God is about a friendship with us–so passionate that he gave us so many signs for us to know his Son when he came to earth.

True or False

	Session 1	Session 2	Session 3	Session 4

Session 1

God created me to be his friend.

Stand up and clasp hands together, like a hand shake.

Session 2

God is holy and takes my sin seriously.

Use arms and hands to make an X across the face.

Session 3

Sin separates me from God.

With arms extended forward in front of their body, hands flexed with fingers pointed upward, take two steps back..

Session 4

God sent Jesus to be the Savior of the world.

Touch palm of right hand with the middle finger of left hand, then repeat the gesture with opposite hands, as in the sign language symbol for Jesus, and point to heaven.

Session 5

God planned for Jesus to pay the price for my sins.

Cross hands over face again as in Truth 2; but then break arms apart and reach up to God like a child who wants to be held reaches up to his father.

Session 6

Session 7

Session 8

SESSION 5
I CAN BE FORGIVEN

SESSION GOALS:
As a result of this session children should be led to:
- Realize that there is nothing they can do to have a friendship with God because of sin.
- Understand that God is willing to forgive sin.
- Affirm that God loves each of us sacrificially and has provided, through Jesus' death on the cross, a payment for sin.
- Believe that they can be forgiven if they are willing to trust in Jesus as their payment for sin.
- Quote scriptures that will help them trust Jesus to forgive them of their sin.

TODAY'S BIG TRUTH: God planned for Jesus to pay the price for my sins.

THE WORLD'S BIG LIE: I am a good person—I can please God.

KEY SCRIPTURES FOR TODAY'S SESSION:
Luke 15:20–22; Romans 3:23; 5:8; 1 John 4:10

MEMORY VERSE: Romans 3:25
Older Children
"For God sent Jesus to take the punishment for our sins and to satisfy God's anger against us. We are made right with God when we believe that Jesus shed his blood, sacrificing his life for us. God was being entirely fair and just when he did not punish those who sinned in former times."

Younger Children
"God sent Jesus to take the punishment for our sins."

LEADERS NEED TO KNOW

Since this is the fifth session with these children, you should know where most of them stand spiritually. Prior to this session, try your best to find out which children in your group have already trusted Christ as Savior and which have not. Naturally, the goal of *True or False* is to lead children to commit their lives to Christ.

You may discover that you are working with older children who have all trusted Christ. If that is true of your group, this session could be an excellent time for review and recommitment.

On the other hand, you may have a young and spiritually immature group who has never had someone lead them through a prayer to trust in Christ. However, your group more than likely will fall between these two extreme possibilities. This is your opportunity to lead your children to commit or recommit their lives to Christ. Be sure you have read all of this leaders guide. Prepare yourself though prayer to witness to the children and watch God work. Remember to be his instrument and leave the results with God.

GEAR UP FOR THE TRUTH
(10 MINUTES)

PREPARE
❑ Write questions from the activity below on 3 x 5-inch cards (one per card). One card per every child. You may repeat the questions, or come up with even more!

PROVIDE
❑ Stickers

❑ 3 x 5-inch cards

❑ White marker board

❑ Dry-erase marker

As the children arrive give them a 3 x 5 card, which asks one of the following questions:
- If you were lost from your family in a mall, what would you do?
- If you were lost in a forest, what would you do?
- If you were lost from your family in a mall, how would you feel?
- If you were lost in a forest, how would you feel?
- How does it feel to be lost?

Ask the children to write down on the back of the card some answers to their question. You could choose to do this activity in small groups with one teacher and have 3–4 groups talking at their tables, or you could do it as one large group. When most of the children have arrived, start the discussion portion of the activity. Talk as a group about the questions. Some children will spontaneously want to tell their stories of being lost. Keep this activity to only ten minutes! End up discussing the last one ("How does it feel to be lost?") Record their answers on the white marker board. Some possible answers are scary, lonely, and afraid. Help the children realize that being lost is not a good thing. Transition to the large group time.

TEACH THE TRUTH

(25 MINUTES)

PREPARE
❏ Make two Bible verse posters: Romans 3:23 and Romans 5:8

PROVIDE
❏ Bibles
❏ Pencils, pens, or felt-tip markers
❏ *True or False* children's workbooks

1. PRAY
Invite God's presence in the room and ask the Holy Spirit to work among every person in the room today.

2. MEMORY VERSE TIME
Guide the children to recall the memory verses previously studied:
- Exodus 34:14
- Romans 3:12
- Romans 3:23
- Romans 6:23
- John 14:6

Award stickers for verses recited.

Introduce the memory verse for today. Guide the children to find Romans 3:25 in their Bibles. For a different twist, have the children call on the adults in the room to quote the verse by memory! Be sure all your children's workers understand this is going to happen. If an adult forgets or stumbles, have the children prompt him or her.

Have children volunteer to explain the verse to the adults.

3. TALK ABOUT SIN

Remind the children that in the sessions the last two weeks we have talked about sin and the results of sin in our lives. Remind them that we have learned that our sin is what separates us from the wonderful friendship with God. God is holy, which means he never does wrong. But when we choose to do wrong things, we turn away from his holiness. That breaks God's heart, because he wants our friendship. That's why our sin is such a big deal to God…and why he had to do something about our sin. That's why he sent Jesus to earth to die for our sins.

4. DISCOVER THE SCRIPTURES

Guide the children to find Romans 5:8 in their Bibles: "But God showed his great love for us by sending Christ to die for us while we were still sinners."

Say: "I truly love this verse because it teaches me:
- God has a great love for me.
- It was God's plan to send Jesus Christ to die for my sins.
- God acted on my behalf even before I wanted forgiveness for my sin."

Say: "Thankfully, God—who is PURE and JUST—is also LOVING and MERCIFUL. After Adam and Eve sinned, God could have chosen to destroy the whole earth and create another planet whose people would not rebel against him. Even though we sinned against him and do not deserve his mercy, he allowed Jesus to die on the cross to pay the price for our sin."

Ask the children to listen carefully, perhaps even close their eyes as you read the verse again slowly. Tell them that you want them to listen to these words with their whole heart. Next, guide the children to look up and read 1 John 4:10: "This is real love. It is not that we loved God, but that he loved us and sent his Son as a sacrifice to take away our sins."

Say: "What Jesus did for us makes it possible for us to be friends with God. Once again, these verses today are reminding us that God really is passionate about a close friendship with us. He really wants to relate to us and to demonstrate his willingness to love us even when it meant sacrificing his only Son."

5. PRESENT GOD'S PLAN

Say: "Unfortunately, Adam and Eve and the people of Noah's day were not the only people who sinned."

A. All people have sinned. In order to become a Christian we must ADMIT to God, and AGREE with God that we have sinned.

Read Romans 3:23 from your visual aid together: "For all have sinned; all fall short of God's glorious standard." Romans 3:23

Ask: "Who has sinned?" Help the children understand that every person has disobeyed God. Some children will readily understand this concept. Some younger children might not. Remember that it is the job of the Holy Spirit to convict and convince people of sin. Discuss this, but do not ask the children for specific examples or make them confess personal sin in front of their peers.

Read from your Bible Roman 6:23: "For the wages of sin is death, but the free gift of God is eternal life through Christ Jesus our Lord."

B. We must BELIEVE and TRUST that God will forgive us because of what Jesus did for us. God knows we have a problem with sin and has provided an answer. God created a plan to forgive us.

Read Romans 5:8 from your visual aid poster. Say: "Really focus on the meaning of these words and look at them as we say the verse once again together."

Say: "God loves us so much that he came down to earth in the person of Jesus Christ and took the punishment for our sins on himself when he died on the cross. Now Jesus wants us to respond to his offer to forgive our sins. God wants us to say, 'I can't do it! I need you to rescue me!'" Illustrate from the parable of the lost son.

Say: "Do you remember where the lost son was? In with the pigs! Let's look at what that lost son in our story did when he realized he was separated from his father, and what his father did. Let's read about this in the Bible."

Read Luke 15:20–21: "So he returned home to his father. And while he was still a long distance away, his father saw him coming. Filled with love and compassion, he ran to his son, embraced him, and kissed him. His son said to him, 'Father, I have sinned against both heaven and you, and I am no longer worthy of being called your son.'"

C. We must turn away, or REPENT, of our sin and TRUST in Jesus' death as our payment for sin.

Say: "When we turn away from sin and reach out to God and ask for forgiveness what will God do? What did the lost boy's father do? (*Ran to his son, embraced him, and kissed him.*) God really will forgive you. He is so happy that you will turn from your sins and trust in the sacrifice of his Son. He will then forgive you and make you his best friend. That is what it means to become a Christian."

Ask: "Do any of you have any questions about how a person becomes a Christian?" Listen to their questions and be willing to answer them.

Say: "Some of you may want to become God's friend and Jesus to become your Savior. If that is true, we would like to know so we can be sure you understand how to become a Christian. This is the most important decision that you can ever make."

6. TIME TO THINK

If you think there are children in your group who are ready to make the commitment to Christ or take another step toward that commitment provide time for them to think quietly. If you have a very young group and there does not seem to be a sufficient comprehension of a commitment at this time, then proceed to the "Apply the Truth to Life" section.

Ask the children to bow their heads and close their eyes for just a little while so they will not be distracted by other people or things in the room.

Say: "Today we are going to break into our groups in a different way. We will not be in our permanent groups. If you would like to talk further about becoming a Christian, after we pray I want you to go to the table with (give the teacher's name)."

You may prefer that these children remain with you and have the other teachers proceed with small groups.

Say: "Before we dismiss I want you to pretend that you are drawing a circle around yourself, and no one but God and you are in your circle. Pray to God about wanting to be his friend. God wants to hear you pray in your own words, but you might want to say something like this: 'Dear God, thank you for sending your Son

Jesus to die on the cross for my sin. I admit that I have sinned and I am sorry. Please forgive me of my sin and make me your friend forever. Thank you, Jesus, for becoming my Savior. Amen.'"

7. PRAY

Thank God for providing a way for our sin to be forgiven. Ask God to reveal himself to the children in your group in a mighty and awesome way.

APPLY THE TRUTH TO LIFE

(25 MINUTES– SMALL-GROUP TIME)

PROVIDE

- Marker board
- Dry-erase markers
- Bibles
- *True or False* children's workbooks

NOTE: This lesson plan provides for those who prayed to trust Christ to be further counseled in a small group. The other children who did not do so can continue with step two in this lesson plan.

1. FURTHER SALVATION INSTRUCTION

Express your happiness over their desire to know more about becoming a Christian. Depending on how you desire to handle children choosing to trust Christ, you will need to adjust to what you would do at this time. For example, you might want the parents of the child to be present when you talk about praying to trust Christ as Savior. Some churches require a parent's permission to proceed with this step. Ask the children if they have any questions about becoming a Christian and try to help clear up anything they may not understand. When the parents arrive to pick up their child, joyfully tell them what transpired and set a time to personally talk again with the child as soon as possible. If only one child responds, ask the parent if now would be a good time to talk.

2. GREET AND REVIEW

Ask: "Do you have any questions you would like to ask me about all that you have heard so far today?" Answer their questions and help the children feel comfortable asking more questions.

Say: "Today we have learned that God wants to forgive us of our sin and he will forgive us because Jesus died to pay the price for our sins. We are going to continue to learn about forgiveness."

3. TODAY'S BIG TRUTH

Review the Big Truths (with motions) presented in former lessons. **Say:** "Today's Big Truth is **God planned for Jesus to pay the price for my sins**." Demonstrate the motion. Ask if anyone can state and demonstrate the motions for all the Big Truths thus far.

4. THE WORLD'S BIG LIE

Say: "So many people do not accept God's forgiveness of their sin because they are not convinced that they need it. The reason is because of the World's Big Lie we are going to learn about today: *'I am a good person—I can please God my way.'* Just like Adam and Eve tried to have a friendship with God their own way, most people today want to do the same thing. What are some of the ways people try to earn God's love?"

Give the children an opportunity to give their answers. The next activity in the workbook will help them understand this concept better.

5. WHY JESUS DIED FOR ME (Workbook page 26)

Have older children work on this page independently first. If you have younger children, do it all together. As a group discuss the answers. Make sure that as you go over the answers you explain why the false ways of thinking will not result in a friendship with God.

Answers:

1. TRUE (Romans 5:8)

2. FALSE (Romans 3:12)

3. FALSE (2 Corinthians 5:10)

4. TRUE (1 Peter 3:18)

5. FALSE (John 6:29)

6. FALSE (Ephesians 2:9)

7. TRUE (Romans 3:22–23)

8. FALSE (Acts 4:12)

6. ADMITTING TO SIN (Workbook page 27)

Call on volunteers to review the story of the lost son as it has been told thus far.

Say: "When we left the lost son last week, he had come to his senses and decided to go back home and ask his father for the job of just being a hired servant. Let's see what the Bible has to tell about what happened next." Read Luke 15:20–22 below, but you may have the children follow along in their workbooks.

"So he returned home to his father. And while he was still a long distance away, his father saw him coming. Filled with love and compassion, he ran to his son, embraced him and kissed him. His son said to him, 'Father, I have sinned against both heaven and you, and I am no longer worthy of being called your son.' But his father said to the servants, 'Quick! Bring the finest robe in the house and put it on him. Get a ring for his finger, and sandals for his feet. '"

Call attention to the first question in their workbooks:
"What did the lost son do right?" (*Admitted that he had sinned.*)

Just like the lost son, we have all run away from God. This Bible story tells us just what to do to enjoy a friendship with God–come to him and admit that we have sinned. When we do that, we are telling God that we believe his way is the right way. We are telling God that having our own selfish way is not right and we admit and agree that he is right. God is pleased when we are willing to turn away from our own selfish ways.

Discuss question 4: How do you think God our heavenly Father will respond to you when you come to him? As the children answer this question in their workbooks, help them see that God will act toward us in the same way the father in this story acted toward his lost son.

7. FORGIVENESS FEELS GOOD! (Workbook page28)
Conclude today's session by reading Psalm 32. Read it aloud with the joy and enthusiasm that it reflects. Guide the children to follow the instructions in their workbooks as they continue to study this passage.

Oh, what joy for those whose rebellion is forgiven
Whose sin is put out of sight!
Yes, what joy for those
Whose record the LORD has cleared of sin,
Whose lives are lived in complete honesty!
When I refused to confess my sin,
I was weak and miserable,
And I groaned all day long.
Day and night your hand of discipline was heavy on me

My strength evaporated like water in the summer heat.
Finally, I confessed all my sins to you
And stopped trying to hide them
I said to myself, "I will confess my rebellion to the LORD."
And you forgave me! All my guilt is gone.

8. PRAY

Thank God for sacrificing his Son on the cross so we can be forgiven and spend eternity with him.

True or False

Session 1	Session 2	Session 3	Session 4
God created me to be his friend.	**God is holy and takes my sin seriously.**	**Sin separates me from God.**	**God sent Jesus to be the Savior of the world.**

Stand up and clasp hands together, like a hand shake.	Use arms and hands to make an X across the face.	With arms extended forward in front of their body, hands flexed with fingers pointed upward, take two steps back..	Touch palm of right hand with the middle finger of left hand, then repeat the gesture with opposite hands, as in the sign language symbol for Jesus, and point to heaven.

Session 5	Session 6	Session 7	Session 8
God planned for Jesus to pay the price for my sins.	**Jesus will never leave me.**		

Cross hands over face again as in Truth 2; but then break arms apart and reach up to God like a child who wants to be held reaches up to his father.	Hug yourself with arms wrapped around body.		

SESSION 6

I CAN BE SURE JESUS WILL ALWAYS LOVE ME

SESSION GOALS:

As a result of this session children should be led to:

- Define and use the word *Incarnation*.
- Believe that God accepts them unconditionally.
- Affirm that God loves them sacrificially.
- Study Scripture that assures them of their salvation.

TODAY'S BIG TRUTH: Jesus will never leave me.

THE WORLD'S BIG LIE: I must work hard to please God on my own.

KEY SCRIPTURES FOR TODAY'S SESSION:

Romans 3:21–25; 27–28

MEMORY VERSE: John 5:24

Older Children

"I assure you, those who listen to my message and believe in God who sent me have eternal life. They will never be condemned for their sins, but they have already passed from death into life."

Younger Children

"Those who listen to my message and believe in God who sent me have eternal life."

LEADERS NEED TO KNOW

The goal of *True or False* is to lead children to place their faith in Jesus Christ. In the last session we presented God's plan for the forgiveness of sin and gave children an opportunity to respond to the gospel. This session reviews God's plan of salvation with more of an emphasis on the assurance of salvation. As a wedding ceremony is the first step of a marriage, praying to accept Christ is just the first step in a lifetime of a personal, intimate relationship with Christ. Unfortunately, many Christians do not fully enjoy a daily, growing, personal friendship with God. God sent Jesus into the world to prove his love for us and to say that he wants to relate to us continually. In today's lesson you will deal with the Big Lie: ***"I must work hard to please God"*** and share the Big Truth: ***Jesus will never leave me.***

Incarnation is the big word that your children will learn today. Many children do not know that Jesus is the eternal God. Young children especially believe that God created the world and that Jesus' life began in the stable in Bethlehem. The children need to know that Jesus has always existed; he is God the Son. Jesus came from splendid heaven to be born in Bethlehem. The Incarnation tells us that God loves us sacrificially. We are so important to God that he went to extraordinary lengths to have a personal relationship with us. He entered our world and became human like us to save us from death.

Children will again be given an opportunity to pray to trust Christ. Perhaps during the last session they gained information they needed but were not ready to pray to trust Christ. It is also possible that some children are not really sure if they have ever trusted Christ. Children from churched homes will often say they have always been Christians. Therefore, this lesson will also include prayers to trust Christ for the first time, to pray for assurance, and to recommit.

GEAR UP FOR THE TRUTH

(10 MINUTES)

PREPARE

❑ An obstacle course with tables, chairs, and other classroom items built in an adjacent room

❑ "Good Works" certificate

❑ "Strong Feelings" certificate

PROVIDE
- ❏ Extra workers for the first 10 minutes
- ❏ Stickers
- ❏ Blindfolds (one for each child)

1. MEMORY VERSE
As children arrive, allow them to recite their memory verse. Award stickers to those who make a serious effort.

2. FEEL YOUR WAY THROUGH
Blindfold each of the children. Tell them that you have set up an obstacle course in an adjacent room and then you or an assistant guide them to the room and explain they are to carefully feel their way through the room and back into the classroom where they began. Assure them that there will be rewards for those who really work hard and trust their feelings of getting back to the other room.

Make sure you have plenty of adults to help make this activity a safe one. Perhaps you can enlist extra youth to be on hand to "spot" the children. Inform the spotters that they are not to give any instruction or help. They are only to prevent injury. A few "running into things" experiences should not hurt the children.

The whole time the children are going through the obstacle course, adult leaders should be taking notes. You might want to actually videotape the children in action! If you do, show an instant replay. Gather children to debrief the experience. **Say:** "The other teachers and I were watching you closely. We think _____ should get the Good Works certificate for working the hardest. (Describe actions the child made that won him/her the reward.) We think _____ should get the Strong Feelings certificate; we could sense that he/she was walking slowly, trying hard not to make any mistakes and really relying on feelings about where things were." Point to more evidence that the child should get the Strong Feelings reward.

TEACH THE TRUTH
(25 MINUTES)

PREPARE
- ❏ A gift for each child. These could be simple. "Dollar stores" or Christian bookstores often have inexpensive items that will be attractive to children. Candy is always a winner. Just be sure to have one for every child. Wrap them like a gift for more fun.

- ❏ If you have not already done so, make arrangements for the celebration that comprises Session 8 of this course (a mere two weeks away!). You will need to arrange

for the appropriate space and audience, enlist adult actors and narrators, assign children's parts, and plan (or enlist someone to plan) the food and fellowship to follow the celebration.

PROVIDE

❑ Marker board

❑ Dry-erase markers

❑ Paper; pens / pencils

1. DISCUSS THE OBSTACLE COURSE ACTIVITY

Ask: "How did you feel when you were involved in the activity?" Most of the children will have felt unsure of themselves. Point out that on the video, or your observations that many of them were walking very cautiously, they were unsure of themselves. Most, if not all, bumped into something; many moved too slowly to finish in time.

Say: "This was a fun activity, but did you know there are some people who truly believe that after they have trusted Jesus to forgive them of their sin, they still must work hard to earn God's love? There are also some people who put all their trust in their own feelings. Today, we are going to learn that God loves us so much that it would be impossible to do anything that would make him love us more. We will also discover that God's love and care are not dependent upon how we feel."

2. I'M WORKING AT IT

Say: "After becoming a Christian, a person wants to please God. That is natural. We all want to please our family and our friends. It feels good to hear one of our parents say, 'I'm proud of you!' or, 'Hey, you did a great job!' So what are some of the things we can do to please God? Don't answer me out loud. Let's have some fun with this one."

Divide the group into two teams. Each team makes a circle and brainstorms ways people can please God. Get the adult leader of the group to help the children come up with a long list. Possible answers include: reading the Bible, praying, caring for the sick, and feeding the hungry, going to church, teaching Sunday school, giving an offering, and worshiping.

Play charades. Have each team take a word from its list and act it out. They can involve as many children as possible in the "act." The other team has to guess what the action to please God is. Play back and forth about 6–8 times as time permits. As each item is guessed, write it on the marker board.

Say: "All the things that you have mentioned are great. In fact, I do a lot of them. They all honor God. Christians will want to do these things. What we as Christians have to be careful about is why we do what we are doing for God."

3. UNCOVER THE BIG LIE

Say: "The reason I said we have to be careful *why* we do these things to please God, is because there is a Big Lie many people believe: ***"I must work hard to please God on my own."*** I have some really good news for you–God loves you! Doing good things to get God to love you will not work. After we become Christians, doing good things so he will keep on loving us will also not work. God wants you to grow more in love with him and live in a way that pleases him, but there is no way that he could love you any more than he already loves you right now! Today's Bible story is going to help us better understand the way we please God."

4. STUDY THE BIBLE – Romans 3:21-28

Guide the children to find the passage in their Bibles. It is so clear in the New Living Translation that it really needs no explanation. Therefore, it is provided for you here in case you do not have the NLT version.

"But now God has shown us a different way of being right in his sight––not by obeying the law but by the way promised in the Scriptures long ago. We are made right in God's sight when we trust in Jesus Christ to take away our sins. And we all can be saved in this same way, no matter who we are or what we have done. For all have sinned; all fall short of God's glorious standard. Yet now God in his gracious kindness declares us not guilty. He has done this through Christ Jesus, who has freed us by taking away our sins. For God sent Jesus to take the punishment for our sins and to satisfy God's anger against us. We are made right with God when we believe that Jesus shed his blood, sacrificing his life for us. God was being entirely fair and just when he did not punish those who sinned in former times. And he is entirely fair and just in this present time when he declares sinners to be right in his sight because they believe in Jesus. Can we boast, then, that we have done anything to be accepted by God? No, because our acquittal is not based on our good deeds. It is based on our faith. So we are made right with God through faith and not by obeying the law."

Say: Last week we learned that Jesus' death on the cross made it possible for us to have a friendship with God. Romans 6:23 says that when people sin, they earn what sin pays–death. But God gives us a free gift–life forever in Christ Jesus. There are seven verses in our session today that teach us about God's free gift. Look at the Scripture and follow the words as I read them."

Normally, it is not a good idea for teachers to read passages this long to children because it may not hold their attention. So prior to the session, practice reading this with great inflection, and know it so well that you sound more like you are telling it as an exciting Bible story rather than reading. Keep eye contact with the children as much as possible and tell this more like a story, which it is.

Read Romans 3:21–28:

"But now God has shown us a different way of being right in his sight – not by obeying the law but by the way promised in the Scriptures long ago. (**Say:** In Old Testament times, boys and girls, God had given the people several laws to obey, but he had promised that one day a Savior would come into the world). We are made right in God's sight when we trust in Jesus Christ to take away our sins. And we all can be saved in this same way, no matter who we are or what we have done.

For all have sinned; all fall short of God's glorious standard. Yet now God in his gracious kindness declares us not guilty. He has done this through Christ Jesus, who has freed us by taking away our sins. For God sent Jesus to take the punishment for our sins and to satisfy God's anger against us. We are made right with God when we believe that Jesus shed his blood, sacrificing his life for us. . . . Can we boast, then, that we have done anything to be accepted by God? No, because our acquittal is not based on our good deeds. It is based on our faith. So we are made right with God through faith and not by obeying the law."

5. INCARNATION – A BIG WORD TO KNOW

Say: "The Bible story tells us that 'God sent Jesus to pay the price for our sins.' Where was Jesus sent from?" Teach them that Jesus is God the Son and he was with him in heaven.

Say: "Jesus was sent from heaven to earth. God in the person of Jesus Christ came from heaven and was born as a baby. That means that God took on human form and lived on earth. We call that

the 'Incarnation.' That's a big word that will impress your parents, so let's say it together: 'Incarnation!'"

For older children, who have studied root words, you can explain that *in* is the root word for "in"! *Carn* is part of the Latin root word for "carne," which means "flesh." So the word *incarnation* means "in the flesh." When Jesus left heaven to come to earth, he put on a physical body like ours so that we could know him.

The very act of God coming into our world proved that God wanted to have a friendship with us. He wants us to get to know him well, and he wants to enjoy being with us in heaven forever.

6. SO WHAT DO YOU DO WITH A FREE GIFT?

Display the gift table. Ask the children if they would like a present? Some will be hesitant; others will be tempted to grab. Watch their reactions. Tell them they can go to the table and select a gift. **Ask**: "So what do you DO when you are offered a free gift?" The children should say in their words, "Accept it." Emphasize "do" because many children will say "thank you." If they respond with "thank you," repeat that is what we say, but what do we do?" **Say:** "God has provided us with the free gift of forgiveness for our sin. Last week we talked about how to become a Christian, and I am sure many of you have been thinking about it this week. This week, we have continued to talk about how Jesus will always love us. Our Bible story concluded with the fact that we are made right with God through trusting in Jesus. And because Jesus is God in the flesh he will never leave us. One day, Jesus will give us heaven. That, too, is a free gift."

7. PRAY

Thank God that he loves us so much that he was willing to put on a body like ours and live on earth so that we could get to know him.

APPLY THE TRUTH TO LIFE

(25 MINUTES–SMALL-GROUP TIME)

PROVIDE

- ❏ *True or False* children's workbooks
- ❏ Pens / pencils; fine-tipped markers
- ❏ Marker board
- ❏ Dry-erase markers

PREPARE

1. GREET AND REVIEW

Welcome the children who arrive at your table. Take time to review the content that has already been covered today. Ask if anyone has any questions about what has been said.

2. TODAY'S BIG TRUTH

Teach today's Big Truth and its corresponding hand motions. The Big truth is: **_Jesus will never leave me._** Review the previous five Big Truths. Call on children to volunteer to say all five big truths by memory. Make this review fun and noncompetitive.

3. HEAVEN IS A FREE GIFT (Workbook page 30).

Say: "When a person prays and asks God to forgive them of their sin, they receive the free gift of eternal life. That means living in heaven with God forever. Isn't that great? You get eternal life the moment you trust in Jesus. You can know that one day you will live in heaven with God forever. That makes living here on earth a lot easier! Let's memorize one of the many Bible verses that teaches us we can be sure that when we die we will live in heaven with Jesus. I like this verse because it is Jesus' very words. I can trust Jesus to tell me the truth. He says:

John 5:24
"I assure you, those who listen to my message and believe in God who sent me have eternal life."

Have children draw a picture in their workbook illustrating what they look forward to seeing in heaven.

4. THE FACTS ABOUT FEELINGS (Workbook page 31)

Say: "We have already discussed that many people think they have to work hard on their own to find ways to please God. We now know that is a big lie. Our memory verse assures us that heaven is a free gift. But another thing that keeps people from truly enjoying a friendship with God is that some people trust their feelings more that the facts in the Bible. Let's name some feelings kids your age have."

As children name feelings, record their answers for everyone to see. The feelings list can be quite extensive. The words they can find in the word search are:

S	**D**	**E**	**T**	**N**	**I**	**O**	**P**	**P**	**A**	**S**	**I**	**D**
H	U	**P**	E	R	**S**	R	T	Y	U	I	O	P
A	N	C	P	K	**G**	**L**	**A**	**D**	S	A	Q	E
L	O	**K**	I	P	H	G	**E**	D	F	G	H	J
D	U	**C**	R	T	U	R	V	**E**	B	N	K	**H**
E	N	**I**	F	U	I	R	F	R	**P**	T	J	**A**
L	J	**S**	P	Y	T	S	P	F	N	**Y**	O	**P**
L	D	**J**	**T**	**I**	**R**	**E**	**D**	P	Y	T	P	**P**
I	C	**O**	R	Y	E	P	**C**	**R**	**A**	**N**	**K**	**Y**
R	F	**Y**	E	N	T	K	U	P	K	G	L	A
H	G	**F**	**E**	**X**	**C**	**I**	**T**	**E**	**D**	S	T	U
T	Y	**U**	C	I	A	C	J	P	U	C	**A**	R
N	O	**L**	R	P	H	B	Y	Z	B	O	G	**D**

Happy   Tired   Sad   Thrilled
Cranky   Glad   Fine   Joyful
Sick   Sleepy   Excited   Disappointed

5. WHAT CAN I DO IF I DO NOT FEEL LIKE I'M FORGIVEN OR GOD IS MY CLOSE FRIEND?

We all have tough days when we do not feel well. Tell children that if they ever are tempted to feel that maybe they are really not saved, they should ask themselves these questions:

• **Have I done something wrong (sinned) and not confessed it to God?**
Just as sin separates us from God before we become Christians, disobeying God after we have become Christians will cause us to feel distant from God again. Next week we are going to talk more about this. If we are aware of sin in our lives, we should pray and confess it to God immediately and do whatever it takes to stay away from that temptation.

• **Am I having a hard time with what is going on in my life right now?**
Sometimes tough situations, like the death of a person we loved very much or the loss of something we need, can cause us to doubt God's love for us. At times like this we need to pray and ask God to help us to trust him no matter what is going on in our life.

•**Am I feeling ill and need to take time to get well?**
God cares about our physical body. He gave us our body and he wants us to take care of it. So if we are feeling bad physically, we must take time to pray and do what doctors tell us to do to get well.

6. I CAN BE SURE (Workbook page 32)

Guide the children to look at the ten statements about what might happen to us once we become a Christian. Some of the statements are absolutely true. The others may have a grain of truth but are not always true. You may have to help the children discern some of these, but it will bring about good discussion. When older children have discovered which statements are always true, have them match the statement to the verse that teaches it is true: 2–D; 4–A; 5–C; 9–B. For younger children, statements 2 and 7 are true.

7. PRESENT AN OPPORTUNITY TO TRUST JESUS

Say: "Last week we gave you an opportunity to pray and ask God to forgive you of sin. Maybe you needed more time to think about making this decision and were not ready to pray last week. Maybe you would feel more comfortable praying in this small group of friends this week. Is there anyone in this group who is ready to pray now?" Give opportunity for response. **Say:** "God would like to hear you pray to him in your own words, but you might want to say something like this:

"Dear God, thank you for sending Jesus from heaven to earth to die on the cross for my sin. Please forgive me of my sin and give me eternal life in heaven with you. Make me the kind of person you want me to be. Help me to please you because you love me so much. In Jesus' name I pray. Amen."

8. PRAY

Thank God for those children who trusted Christ today.

True or False

Session 1	Session 2	Session 3	Session 4

God created me to be his friend.

Stand up and clasp hands together, like a hand shake.

God is holy and takes my sin seriously.

Use arms and hands to make an X across the face.

Sin separates me from God.

With arms extended forward in front of their body, hands flexed with fingers pointed upward, take two steps back..

God sent Jesus to be the Savior of the world.

Touch palm of right hand with the middle finger of left hand, then repeat the gesture with opposite hands, as in the sign language symbol for Jesus, and point to heaven.

Session 5	Session 6	Session 7	Session 8

God planned for Jesus to pay the price for my sins.

Cross hands over face again as in Truth 2; but then break arms apart and reach up to God like a child who wants to be held reaches up to his father.

Jesus will never leave me.

Hug yourself with arms wrapped around body.

When I trust in Jesus, God makes me his child.

Form arms as if rocking a baby.

SESSION 7
GROWING UP IN GOD'S FAMILY

SESSION GOALS:
As a result of this session children should be led to:
- Understand that becoming a Christian makes them a child of God.
- Feel that God truly understands them and their particular life situation.
- Trust that God will always be a part of their lives.
- Realize that heaven is their home.

TODAY'S BIG TRUTH: When I trust in Jesus, God makes me his child.

THE WORLD'S BIG LIE: God and the church are fine—when I have the time.

KEY SCRIPTURE FOR TODAY'S SESSION:
Luke 15:22–24; Romans 5:5; Philippians 4:6; Hebrews 4:14–16; 1 John 5:14

MEMORY VERSE: John 1:12
Older Children
"But to all who believed him and accepted him, he gave the right to become children of God."

Younger Children
"But to all who believed him and accepted him, he gave the right to become children of God."

True or False

LEADERS NEED TO KNOW

Becoming a Christian is a life-changing, miraculous work of God. We are adopted into the family of God. God wants us to be more than friends; he wants us to become a member of the family. The Big Truth we will teach today is *When I trust in Jesus, God makes me his child*. Through this session we want to help children realize that as Christians they have all the rights and privileges of a family member. Being in the family provides a child with security and relationships.

We all long for someone to understand and identify with us. Jesus, who became flesh for us, experienced the ups and downs of life as a human baby, child, teenager, and man. As God, Christ understood his creation perfectly, but by becoming a human being, Jesus let us know how intimately and completely he understands us. Jesus knows all about our temptations and weaknesses as well as our joys and strengths. We have a God who really wants to walk with us, just as he was able to walk with Adam and Eve in the garden.

We, children included, tend to compartmentalize our lives and relationships. We have our social activities, play, work, school, piano lessons, church, extended families, etc. Many of our children have church friends, neighborhood friends, and school friends, all of which never intersect. God does not want to be another relationship among all the other relationships or compartments in our busy lives. He wants to be a part of every hour of every day. God wants to demonstrate that he understands us intimately. The challenge of this session is to help children integrate their relationship with God into the fabric of their lives.

Because of the Incarnation, Jesus let us know he understands firsthand every feeling we have. Teaching this concept will help children develop a personal relationship with God. Be alert to help children understand that God is a person, not an idea or concept.

God not only understands us intimately; he wants to relate to us continually. Each of us will always be a beloved child of God, and because of his Holy Spirit we can always count on his indwelling presence. God's relationship with us begins when we trust Christ and will continue into eternity. Heaven is our home. Jesus told us plainly, "I am going to prepare a place for you . . . . When everything is ready, I will come and get you, so that you will always be with me where I am" (John 14:2–3).

GEAR UP FOR THE TRUTH
(10 MINUTES)

PREPARE

❑ Invite a couple with a new baby in your church to visit for about 15 minutes in your classroom. They should be present for at least five minutes prior to the session and be present for the first ten minutes of the session.

❑ If you have not already done so, make final arrangements for the celebration that comprises Session 8 of this course. You will need to arrange for the appropriate space and audience, enlist adult actors and narrators, assign children's parts, and plan (or enlist someone to plan) the food and fellowship to follow the celebration.

PROVIDE

❑ Three large sheets of tag board (optional: poster board, or craft paper cut into 3–4' lengths)

❑ Broad tip felt markers

1. MEMORY VERSE

As children arrive, allow them to say their memory verse and receive a sticker.

2. INVITE A FAMILY

Invite a couple with an infant to arrive before your class begins. Children love to see babies, so have the couple "show off" their baby to the children and talk about the baby. After most of the children have arrived call their attention to the three large sheets of tag board. Divide the children into three groups to brainstorm and report back to the group the answer to this question, "What do families do for babies?" Each group should choose someone to write their list of answers on the tag board. Each group should choose someone else to be the reporter. Give the groups 4–5 minutes to complete their work. Each group should also have an adult leader with them.

The couple with their baby should just keep interacting with the baby to meet its needs. If you are working with younger children, you might have the father and mother first talk about things they do for their baby. Younger children may also need to have the adult leader record their answers on the tag board.

Call the whole group together. Perhaps the mother or father of the baby could lead the reporting session. Let each group report their findings. They should include, feeding, clothing, bathing, changing the baby's diaper, playing, showing love, cuddling, singing, taking the baby to the doctor, etc. Ask the parents to add to the list. Be sure that a growing relationship with the baby, security, a home to live in, and money to buy what the baby needs, are included. Ask the parents what other future things they look forward to providing their child. These could include education, baseball games, piano lessons, etc. As they speak, an adult should add these to the list.

Conclude by reading John 1:12: "But to all who believed him and accepted him, he gave the right to become children of God." Point out that the baby before them is helpless to cook its own food or take a bath. In fact, the baby is totally dependent upon the parents.

Say: "God planned for parents to meet the needs of their children. The parent–child relationship was given to us by God so that we could understand the close relationship he wants to have with us. God wants us to understand how much he cares for us and wants to meet our needs.

Thank the family for visiting the classroom and helping us get started today. They may leave at this point.

3. PRAY
Thank God for giving us the right to become his children.

TEACH THE TRUTH
(25 MINUTES)

PREPARE
- Label one large bag "NEEDS" and one "WANTS"
- Posters titled: "What the Lost Son Needed" and "What the Father Provided"
- Visual aid of the John 1:12 passage
- The words of John 1:12 written individually on index cards; place one under each child's chair

PROVIDE
❏ Half sheets of colored paper–two colors; one of each color for every child
❏ Pens/pencils or thin felt-tipped markers
❏ Tape

1. NEEDS OR WANTS
Call attention to the two "Needs" and "Wants" bags you have prepared. **Say:** "God has promised to meet all our needs. He may even supply some of our wants. It is important that we know the difference."

Give each child two pieces of paper of two different colors. Ask them to write an example of a need on one color and a want on the other. Have the children place their answers in the bag they think is correct. After all the children have placed their answers in the bags, go through the Want bag and discuss the answers. If some of the ideas are actually needs, move them to the Needs bag. Go through the same process with your Needs bag. Help children understand the difference between wants and needs

2. STUDY THE BIBLE—1 John 5:14
Say: "We have already talked about the fact that a parents should care for all the needs of their child. God is the perfect parent. We can trust him to care for all our needs. That is why we are told in Philippians 4:6, 'Don't worry about anything; instead, pray about everything. Tell God what you need, and thank him for all he has done.'"

Say: Parents don't just want to supply what their child needs; most parents want to give their child wonderful experiences and many good things that will make their life fulfilling. It gives parents great happiness to be able to give good things to their children. Did you know that it brings God great pleasure to give good gifts to his children? Did you know that God will also supply some of our wants that fit within his plan for us? Yes, he will! The Bible says in 1 John 5:14–15, 'And we can be confident that he will listen to us whenever we ask him for anything in line with his will. And if we know he is listening when we make our requests, we can be sure that he will give us what we ask for.'

"Did you catch the words, 'in line with his will'? God knows us better than we know ourselves. He knows all about us. He knows what will really be best for us. So if we ask him for something that is not best for us, it is not in line with his will for us. God will not give us something that will hurt us or our friendship with him. When God answers a prayer of ours by saying no, we need trust that he really does know what is best for us. We need to be thankful that he understands us.

"Jesus told his disciples that if fathers in this world liked to give good things to their children, that our heavenly Father would want to give good gifts to his children even more. Can you imagine how much more God would love to give good gifts to each of us? The Bible teaches us that God delights in blessing his very own children. Let's see an example of this as we return to the story of the lost son."

3. BACK TO THE STORY OF THE LOST SON—Luke 15:22-24

Review the story as it has been shared thus far in former sessions. Then guide the children to open their Bibles to Luke 15:22–24. With great enthusiasm, read this scripture from the Bible. For the sake of clarity, we suggest the NLT version:

"But his father said to the servants, 'Quick! Bring the finest robe in the house and put it on him. Get a ring for his finger, and sandals for his feet. And kill the calf we have been fattening in the pen. We must celebrate with a feast, for this son of mine was dead and has now returned to life. He was lost, but now he is found!' So the party began."

On a visual aid poster, title a list: "What the Lost Son Needed." Ask the children to think of what the lost son really needed. Record these on your visual aid. Answers should include: food, water, a place to stay, a job, and forgiveness. Title another poster: "What the Father Provided." Have the children study the Bible passage to list what the father gave his son. Answers should include: finest robe in the house, a ring, and sandals, a fatted calf for a feast, a big party, and forgiveness. Make a big deal about the extravagant love of the Father.

Say: "The father in this story represents God in heaven. He truly wants to delight in his children. He wants to bless us. He wants to give us good things. But just like the lost son, until we come to the Father, we cannot receive all that he wants to lavish on us.

"Just like the father in the story of the lost son celebrated when his son came home, that's exactly what God does when we trust in Jesus. He celebrates! We

were lost and away from him, but now are found. We were dead, but now we are alive. We were his enemy, but now we are his friends.

"God celebrates because he knows that one day he will welcome us into heaven to live with him forever. He's preparing a place for us in heaven so that we will be able to enjoy him up close. We'll live with him there forever. The Bible tells us all sorts of wonderful things about heaven. There are streets of gold and gates of pearls. And while those things will be beautiful to see, the best part of heaven will be living with God forever."

4. LEARN THE MEMORY VERSE—John 1:12

Ask the children to find John 1:12 in their Bibles: ***"But to all who believed him and accepted him, he gave the right to become children of God."*** Because there might be many Bible translations present in your classroom, show a visual aid of this Scripture taken from the NLT version. Tell the children that this is the last memory verse they will have for this study. Give them a few minutes to try to commit it to memory. Then remove the visual aid from their sight. Have the children try to say the verse in unison.

Then ask the children to feel under their chair to see if they can find a word hidden there. Every child should find an index card with a word on it. (There are 19 words including the reference. So if at all possible make this an activity everyone can have a part in. If you have fewer than 19 children, the teachers can have the extra words. If you have more children, print out two copies of the verse on two different colors of paper. Make two teams that will find the words, on two different colored papers. Then race to see which team can put its verse together first.) After it seems like all the words have been found, ask the children to mix around the room getting the words of the verse in order.

5. THE RIGHT TO ENJOY GOD FOREVER

Say: "Our memory verse today says that God gives us the right to become his very own children. Not only does God want a relationship with each of us, he wants that relationship with us to last forever.

"At the right time in history Jesus came to earth. His disciples could touch him and talk with him. They enjoyed being with him. Then Jesus told them of God's plan. They learned that Jesus would die on a cross. They became sad because they knew they would miss him. Jesus told them that they would not have to be sad. God the Father had a great plan. All people who believed in Jesus as the Son of God would have his Holy Spirit living in their heart. That way we could always have God's love with us wherever we are, at any time of the day. I want to show you another Bible verse, Romans 5:5. 'For we know how dearly God loves us, because he has given us the Holy Spirit to fill our hearts with his love.'

"So where is Jesus right now?"
(The children should answer, "He is here with us!")

6. PRAY
Thank God that he offers us a friendship that lasts forever.

APPLY THE TRUTH TO LIFE
(25 MINUTES–SMALL-GROUP TIME)

PROVIDE
❑ Bibles

❑ *True or False* children's workbooks

❑ Pens/ pencils, or fine-tipped markers

1. GREET AND REVIEW
Say: "I hope that you have felt good about being a part of this group for the last six weeks, and I hope you are looking forward to our time together today. It is part of God's plan that Christians spend time together. God wants us to worship him, study the Bible, and just have a great time together. All of God's children are a part of one big family. That is why being with other members of your church is so important. In the same way that God designed babies to need people to help them grow, in a church all of us are to help each other grow to know more about God. That is what this small-group time is especially designed to do. We have spent time learning about God together, and we have enjoyed each other's fellowship.

2. TODAY'S BIG TRUTH
Say: "Our Big Truth for today is ***When I trust in Jesus, God makes me his child.*** Guide the children to find page 33 in their *True or False Workbook*. Have them make the motions corresponding to the Big Truth.

Tell the children that the next session, which will be the last study session of *True or False*, will be a review of all they have learned. Inform the children that they will have an audience for the review, since most of the review will be a dramatic reading. Let them know you want all of them to participate. Take time to review all eight of the Big Truths, which they'll perform in the drama. Carefully practice all the motions. As you practice these, watch for children who seem to be able to handle more responsibility.

3. CHILDREN'S RIGHTS (Workbook page 34)

Review the memory verse on the top of the page. Talk to the children about the different rights, privileges, and things they receive by becoming a child of God then ask children to answer the question at the top of the page. There are multiple answers to this question. Answers could include: forgiveness of sin, a home or mansion in heaven, answers to prayer, friendship with God, peace, etc. Guide children to think of five things they want to list and thank God for.

4. ASSIGN DRAMA PARTS

All the leaders in the study should read the drama before class and as a group decide who can best do the parts of the dramatic reading. At this time assign the children's parts.

5. GOD UNDERSTANDS (Workbook pages 34 and 35)

Read Hebrews 4:14–16. Tell students that this Bible passage helps us learn that God understands us. Explain that a high priest in the Old Testament represented God to the people and the people to God. Tell the children that the only High Priest we need is Jesus himself. Work together as a group as you guide the children through discussion to fill in the blanks.

6. CAN YOU HELP? (Workbook page 35)

Say: Most people would never say anything bad about God or about being a part of a church. In fact, they might even say some very good things about Jesus. But they still believe the world's Big Lie: *'God and the church are fine—when I have the time."*

Read each case study and guide your students to think of ways to help the children in each scenario. **Ask** them, "Can you help Andrew, Jessica, Colin, and Sarah?"

JESSICA

Jessica got all her homework done early and played with her friends until sup-pertime. After supper she stayed on the phone until time for her bath and bed-time. Was she ever tired! Her dad came by her room and said, "Jessica, have you read your Bible and devotion for today?" Oops! She knew she had not. Jessica thinks, "Can't God understand I'm tired?"

What should Jessica do? _____

Why? _____

COLIN

Colin has a best friend he likes to spend time with. Colin's family is faithful to attend church, but his friend's family does not have a church. They plan the coolest things to do on Sundays, and often invite Colin to go along. At first Colin did not ask his parents if he could go; he just thought they would say no, but now he is wondering why he could not go at least once a month.

What should Colin do? _____

Why? _____

SARAH

Sarah loves to just stay at home. She likes to read, cook, sleep late, and play with her toys. This Sunday morning her mother walked into her room and told her it was time to get up and get ready for church. Her grandparents called and are on their way already. Sarah doesn't feel like getting out of bed. "Anyway," she thinks, "my parents stay home so why do I need to go to church?"

What should Sarah do? _____

Why? _____

7. PRAY

Thank God for allowing us to be his children and loving us as a Father.

True or False

Session 1	Session 2	Session 3	Session 4

God created me to be his friend.

Stand up and clasp hands together, like a hand shake.

God is holy and takes my sin seriously.

Use arms and hands to make an X across the face.

Sin separates me from God.

With arms extended forward in front of their body, hands flexed with fingers pointed upward, take two steps back..

God sent Jesus to be the Savior of the world.

Touch palm of right hand with the middle finger of left hand, then repeat the gesture with opposite hands, as in the sign language symbol for Jesus, and point to heaven.

Session 5	Session 6	Session 7	Session 8

God planned for Jesus to pay the price for my sins.

Cross hands over face again as in Truth 2; but then break arms apart and reach up to God like a child who wants to be held reaches up to his father.

Jesus will never leave me.

Hug yourself with arms wrapped around body.

When I trust in Jesus, God makes me his child.

Form arms as if rocking a baby.

God celebrates when I come back to him.

Begin by clapping hands then raise arms, palms up and hands raised to God.

SESSION 8
CELEBRATE!

SESSION GOALS:
As a result of this session children should be led to:
- Understand that when a person becomes a Christian, God celebrates.
- Review the concepts, Big Truths, and scriptures they have learned through this study.
- Present what they have learned to their parents, families, or another group.
- Celebrate!

TODAY'S BIG TRUTH: God celebrates when I come back to him.

THE WORLD'S BIG LIE: None

KEY SCRIPTURES FOR TODAY'S SESSION:
Exodus 34:14; Luke 15:11–24;
Romans 3:12, 23; 3:25; 6:23; John 1:12; 5:24; 14:6

LEADERS NEED TO KNOW

This session is designed to be a review of the Big Truths, concepts, and Scripture the children have studied through the *True or False* series. Children will participate in an Incarnation celebration drama written for children. While participating in the dramatic reading, reviewing the story of the lost son, and reciting scriptures, they will be reinforcing the truths they have learned. Ideally, their parents should be invited to the presentation so they can demonstrate to their parents what they have learned. If for some reason, it's not possible to have their parents present, invite another group to become the audience for the children's presentation. If you have several age groups of children working through this curriculum, perhaps the oldest group could present this to the younger group; for example, the fifth and sixth graders could present this to the first and second graders.

PREPARE

While there will not be any new content for this session, there will be preparation that should be done well in advance. Listed below is a preparation schedule.

BEFORE THE PRESENTATION

❑ Determine whom the audience will be.

❑ Send out invitations to the selected audience. They are to arrive the last half of your session.

❑ Enlist two men in your church comfortable with drama to dress as the lost son and the father in the story. Give them a copy of the dramatic reading, and secure biblical costumes for them or ask them to come up with simple Biblical costumes. Record your actors below.

❑ Determine if the classroom space you are using will be adequate for the number of guests you will have. If you will need a larger space, reserve that room, or make whatever arrangements you need to at this time.

❑ Select the actors.

The father will be played by _____

The lost son will be played by_____

❑ Select Narrators 1 and 2. The majority of the dramatic reading will be done by these two adults. You will want to select people who can project and be dramatic in their reading. They can be the teachers, other adults, or older youth. Record your narrators below.

Narrator 1 _____

Narrator 2 _____

❑ Plan with those assisting you what will be done for the fellowship time at the end of the session. You may want the celebration to be a pizza party with soft drinks, or you may simply choose to have cookies and lemonade. (Or go along with the biblical theme and bring in the fatted calf!) Discuss with your other teachers who will bring what. Don't forget the paper goods! And be sure to include your audience in the fellowship.

<u>Before the presentation</u> assign all the children's parts:

Child 1 _____

Child 2 _____

Child 3 _____

Child 4 _____

Child 5 _____

Child 6 _____

Child 7 _____

Child 8 _____

GEAR UP FOR THE TRUTH
(30 MINUTES)

1. PREPARE WITH THE CHILDREN

As children arrive, have them help you prepare for the celebration. They can put tablecloths on the table, arrange cookies, and whatever else you may need to have done. When it is time to start the session, gather the children into the large group and rehearse the dramatic reading of **"The Father Celebrates."** Reading through this should take 18 minutes, so if all the parts are pre-assigned and all the participants, including the lost son and the father, are all present on time, you should be able to get one rehearsal in. Remember, the value of this activity is the review and the acting out of all eight Big Truths together. The presentation does not need to be a polished production, but a sincere, heartfelt learning experience.

Place each participant where they will stand during the presentation. The father and the lost son should be visible and yet separate from the children. It would be ideal if they could be on a raised platform. The narrators could stand central to the focal area with children #1–4 on one side and children #5–8 on the other side. The rest of the children could be grouped equally behind the eight children who have individual parts. Ask the children who have individual parts to take one large step forward before they speak.

The children will be using their workbooks, since the script for the dramatic reading is included on pages 38–45. Show them how to stand and hold the book attractively. Tell them not to cover their faces with the book as they read. When the children read Scripture as a group, they will all be quoting the memory verses they should have learned. Ask them to try to look up at the audience when they quote the Scripture.

2. PRAY

Right before you open the door and invite the audience into your classroom, lead the children in prayer, asking that God bless this time and use it to bring others to know him.

TEACH THE TRUTH
(30 MINUTES)

1. WELCOME THE PARENTS AND INTRODUCE THE CELEBRATION

Welcome your guests to the class and invite them all to find a place to sit. **Say:** "During the last seven weeks our children have been learning some of the most important Big Truths in the Bible. Through many of our sessions, we have also learned about the story of the Lost Son. Today, we would like for you to experience the Bible Verses, stories, and Big Truths we have discovered."

THE FATHER CELEBRATES

Narrator 1: You are about to hear a love story. It's about the love God has for us as his creation and everything God did to have a friendship with us.

Narrator 2: Our story is wrapped around a Bible passage you probably know as the parable of the Lost Son.

All Kids: We were CREATED FOR GOD.

Child 1: "So God created people in his own image; God patterned them after himself; male and female he created them" (Genesis 1:27).

Narrator 1: In the very beginning, God created everything. He made a perfect place for people to live and called it the Garden of Eden. They had everything they needed.

Narrator 2: There Adam and Eve lived and enjoyed their friendship with God. They talked to him like they talked to each other. They walked with him in the Garden. They laughed together and enjoyed the beautiful trees, flowers and playful animals.

Narrator 1: Adam and Eve enjoyed God's love. They were joyful. They were at peace.

Narrator 2: God enjoyed Adam and Eve. He was glad he created them. He loved them very much.

True or False

All Kids: The Big Truth is, **God created me to be his friend.** (*Children should stand up and clasp their hands together, like a handshake.*)

All Kids: "You must worship no other gods, but only the LORD, for he is a God who is passionate about his relationship with you" (Exodus 34:14).

Narrator 1: God is passionate about his friendship with us! What a thrilling thought that the God who created the whole universe cares for me and wants my friendship.

Narrator 2: If only life had stayed that simple. But one sad day, Adam and Eve chose to disobey God. God gave them just one rule, and they disobeyed that rule. Disobedience to God is called sin.

All Kids: SIN DESTROYS MY FRIENDSHIP WITH GOD.

Narrator 1: Jesus once told a story about a man who had two sons. The younger son told his father...

Son: I want my share of your estate now, instead of waiting until you die.

Narrator 2: (*Father pantomimes this action.*) So his father agreed to divide his wealth between his sons.

Narrator 1: When the son asked for his father's money, he was saying, "Father, I want nothing to do with you. I don't want you as my father. In fact, I wish you were dead."

Narrator 2: The son took the money and ran away from home.

Narrator 1: We are all like that son in the story. We have all run away from God, our father. We've run away from God, our greatest friend. We did that by failing to keep God's rules about loving him and others.

All Kids: "All have turned away from God; all have gone wrong. No one does good, not even one" (Romans 3:12).

Child 1: We disobey our parents.

Child 2:	We fight with our brothers and sisters.
Child 3:	We don't share and refuse to help others.
Child 4:	We lie and steal.
Child 5:	We cheat in school and at games.
Child 6:	We speak unkind and often bad words.
Child 7:	We do not trust Jesus to forgive us of our sin.
Child 8:	We run away from our Father God.
Narrator 2:	Sin hurts us. It hurts other people. And it breaks God's heart. God wants to be friends with each of us. But the wrong things we do make it impossible for us to be God's friends.
Child 2:	Habakkuk 1:13 says, "Your eyes are too pure to look on evil; you cannot tolerate wrong (NIV)."
Narrator 1:	God is holy, which means he never does wrong. But when we choose to do wrong things, we turn away from him. That breaks God's heart, because he wants our friendship. That's why our sin is such a big deal to God.
All Kids:	The Big Truth is, **God is holy and takes my sin seriously.** *(Cross arms in front of face.)*
Narrator 2:	Sin leaves us feeling lost and alone and away from God.
All Kids:	We are LOST AND ALONE BECAUSE OF SIN.
Narrator 1:	We all have the very same problem. We have all failed God.
All Kids:	"For all have sinned; all fall short of God's glorious standard" (Romans 3:23).
Narrator 2:	Remember the lost son? He was secure while he lived with his father. Listen to what happened to him when he ran away from his father.

True or False

Narrator 1: *(Son acts this out as it is read.)* A few days later this younger son packed all his belongings and took a trip to a distant land, and there he wasted all his money on wild living. About the time his money ran out, a great famine swept over the land, and he began to starve. He persuaded a local farmer to hire him to feed his pigs. The boy became so hungry that even the pods he was feeding the pigs looked good to him. But no one gave him anything.

Narrator 2: Sin creates a huge problem between God and us. God says that when we sin, we are lost and alone. Sin takes us far away from God. It separates us from him. Let's act out what it means to be separated from God.

Act out with "all kids" the demonstration from session 3. Have one adult in the middle wearing sign that says "God." All kids should gather closely around him or her—in a group hug. **Ask:** *"How close are we now?" (They should answer, very close or all together.) Have everyone take one step back.* **Say:** *"That's what happens to us when we sin." Step back again.* **Say:** *"Each time we sin, we get further and further away from God. None of us can reach him. We can't reach each other." Keep taking one step back until no one can stretch a hand out to "God" or to anyone else.*

All Kids: The Big Truth is, **Sin separates me from God.**
(With arms extended forward palms out with fingers pointed upward, take two steps back, as if pushing away.)

Narrator 1: When we sin, we are separated from God. No one else can rescue us—not our friends, not our parents, not our pastor, not any human being. And there's nothing we can do to rescue ourselves. The wrong things we do have taken us so far away that we are lost and alone and can't find our way back to God.

Narrator 2: The Bible calls that painful kind of separation "death." When someone's body dies, we're completely cut off from that person. That's physical death. But there's another kind of death that is even worse. "Spiritual death" is when people are far from God.

All Kids: "For the wages of sin is death" (Romans 6:23).

Narrator 2: Separation from God is the result of sin. That sounds bad–and it is.

Narrator 1: We're lost and alone. Who is going to help us?

All Kids: JESUS IS THE ONE AND ONLY SAVIOR.

Narrator 2: Acts 4:12 tells us that Jesus is the only one who can save us. His name is the only power in the world that has been given to redeem his lost and alone people. He is our only hope.

All Kids: Jesus says, "I am the way, the truth, and the life. No one can come to the Father except through me" (John 14:6).

Narrator 1: God wanted us to be able to recognize the one he sent to save us. So God gave us three special ways to be sure that Jesus is the world's one-and-only Savior.

Child 3: Because Jesus fulfilled hundreds of Old Testament prophecies, we could be sure he was born to be our Savior.

Child 4: Because Jesus performed miracles, we could be sure he was God in the flesh.

Child 5: Because Jesus rose from the dead, we could be sure he was God's chosen One–and that he had paid for our sins in full.

Narrator 2: Some people say there are lots of ways to be friends with God. But Jesus is the world's one-and-only Savior.

All Kids: The Big Truth is, **God sent Jesus to be the Savior of the world.** *(Touch palm of each hand alternately with the middle finger, as the sign language symbol for Jesus, then point to heaven with the right hand.)*

Narrator 1: Remember the lost son? Well, he finally came to his senses. He said to himself,

Lost Son: At home even the hired men have food enough to spare, and here I am, dying of hunger! I will go home to my father and say, "Father, I have sinned against both heaven and you, and I am no longer worthy of being called your son. Please take me on as a hired man."

Narrator 2: The lost son did a really smart thing. He recognized that there was one place he could get help–his father. He needed to be forgiven for running away from his father. Would his father help him? Would his father forgive him? Can we be forgiven?

All Kids: I CAN BE FORGIVEN!

Narrator 1: Our heavenly Father wants us to recognize that there is only one place we can get help. God has a plan to bring us to himself and make us friends with him.

All Kids: The Big Truth is, **God sent Jesus to pay the price for my sin.** (*Cross hands over face, then break arms apart and reach up to God as a child wanting to be held.*)

Narrator 1: If we want to be friends with God, our sin must be dealt with. And we can't do that ourselves. There's only one way to do it. When Jesus died on the cross, he died for all of our sins. He did something we can't do. Only Jesus could pay the price for our sin, and that's exactly what Jesus did.

All Kids: "For God sent Jesus to take the punishment for our sins and to satisfy God's anger against us. We are made right with God when we believe that Jesus shed his blood, sacrificing his life for us" Romans 3:25.

Narrator 2: The death of Jesus on the cross makes it possible for us to be friends of God.

Child 6: Romans 5:8 says, "But God showed his great love for us by sending Christ to die for us while we were still sinners."

Narrator 2: That's Good News. But our lost son is still stuck with the pigs. What about him?

Narrator 1: The lost son returned home to his father. And while he was still a long distance away, his father saw him coming. Filled with love and compassion, he ran to his son, embraced him, and kissed him. His son said to him,

Lost Son: Father, I have sinned against both heaven and you, and I am no longer worthy of being called your son.

Narrator 2:   The son ran home to his father.

Narrator 1:   God wants us to run home to him by trusting in the death of Jesus for the forgiveness of our sins. And when we do, God comes running to us.

Narrator 2:   We cannot save ourselves from our sin and become friends with God by anything we do.

Narrator 1:   We need a miracle to happen—and that's exactly what God does. God performs a miracle that will last forever.

All Kids: I CAN BE SURE JESUS WILL ALWAYS LOVE ME.

Narrator 2:   There is nothing that I can do that will cause Jesus to love me more.

All Kids: The Big Truth is, **Jesus will never leave me.**
(Hug self with arms wrapped around.)

Narrator 1:   We have a friendship with God because we have faith in Jesus. We will live forever in heaven because Jesus will never leave us.

All Kids: Jesus said, "I assure you, those who listen to my message and believe in God who sent me have eternal life" (John 5:24).

Narrator 2:   When we trust in Jesus, and God is our Father, we have a new, big family.

All Kids: It is so much fun to be GROWING UP IN GOD'S FAMILY.

Child 7:   God my Father understands me, and he understands you!

Child 8:   God my Father will love me always!

All Kids: The Big Truth is: **When I trust in Jesus, God makes me his child.** *(Form arms as if rocking a baby.)*

Narrator 1:   God doesn't just want us to be his friends; he wants us to be a part of his family. We become God's son or daughter.

All Kids: "But to all who believed him and accepted him, he gave the right to become children of God" (John 1:12).

Narrator 2: There is another Big Truth to this wonderful story.

Narrator 1: Let's hear the Father tell us in his own words!

Father: (Said to the servants,) Quick! Bring the finest robe in the house and put it on him. Get a ring for his finger, and sandals for his feet. And kill the calf we have been fattening in the pen. We must celebrate with a feast, for this son of mine was dead and has now returned to life. He was lost, but now he is found.

All Kids: The Big Truth is, God celebrates when I come back to him! (Clap hands; then raise arms, palms up.)

Narrator 1: So the party began.

Narrator 2: That's exactly what God does for us when we trust in Christ. He celebrates. We were lost, but now we are found. We were dead but are now alive. We were his enemy, but now we are his friends, and we will live together with God and his people in heaven forever.

Narrator 1: Let's hear those Big Truths again:

All kids: (Say the eight Big Truths in unison with the motions.)
1. God created me to be his friend.

2. God is holy and takes my sin seriously.

3. Sin separates me from God.

4. God sent Jesus to be the Savior of the world.

5. God sent Jesus to pay the price for my sin.

6. Jesus will never leave me.

7. When I trust in Jesus, God makes me his child.

8. God celebrates when I come back to him.

2. CONCLUDE THE PRESENTATION

Thank the children for their participation and the adults for their help. Thank the audience for their attendance and attention. Tell of the plans for the following celebration and invite everyone to stay and participate.

3. PRAY

Thank God for this time of learning with the children. Ask him to bless what they have learned through his Word. Ask God to bless the time of fellowship and food that will follow.

4. LET THE PARTY BEGIN!

BIBLE VERSES TO KNOW
FOR OLDER CHILDREN

Session 1
❏ Exodus 34:14   "You must worship no other gods, but only the LORD, for he is a God who is passionate about his relationship with you."

Session 2
❏ Romans 3:12   "All have turned away from God; all have gone wrong. No one does good, not even one."

Session 3
❏ Romans 3:23   "For all have sinned; all fall short of God's glorious standard."

❏ Romans 6:23   "For the wages of sin is death, but the free gift of God is eternal life through Christ Jesus our Lord."

Session 4
❏ John 14:6   "Jesus told him, 'I am the way, the truth, and the life. No one can come to the Father except through me.' "

Session 5
❏ Romans 3:25   "For God sent Jesus to take the punishment for our sins and to satisfy God's anger against us. We are made right with God when we believe that Jesus shed his blood, sacrificing his life for us. God was being entirely fair and just when he did not punish those who sinned in former times."

Session 6
❏ John 5:24   "I assure you, those who listen to my message and believe in God who sent me have eternal life. They will never be condemned for their sins, but they have already passed from death into life."

Session 7
❏ John 1:12   "But to all who believed him and accepted him, he gave the right to become children of God."

Permission is granted to duplicate this page for parents

BIBLE VERSES TO KNOW FOR YOUNGER CHILDREN

Session 1

❑ Exodus 34:14   "God who is passionate about his relationship with you."

Session 2

❑ Romans 3:12   "All have turned away from God; all have gone wrong."

Session 3

❑ Romans 3:23   "For all have sinned; all fall short of God's glorious standard."

❑ Romans 6:23   "The free gift of God is eternal life through Christ Jesus our Lord."

Session 4

❑ John 14:6   "Jesus told him, 'I am the way, the truth, and the life.' "

Session 5

❑ Romans 3:25   "God sent Jesus to take the punishment for our sins."

Session 6

❑ John 5:24   "Those who listen to my message and believe in God who sent me have eternal life."

Session 7

❑ John 1:12   "But to all who believed him and accepted him, he gave the right to become children of God."

Permission is granted to duplicate this page for parents

BIG WORDS TO LEARN

HOLY

Perfect in every way; set apart for God; pure. God is holy.

MIRACLES

Wonderful things that only God can do. Jesus did many miracles to prove that he is God. For example, Jesus calmed a storm on the Sea of Galilee, he fed 5,000 people with a little boy's lunch, and he made blind people see.

PASSIONATE

Caring about something so much that we put all our thought and energy into it.

PROPHECY

Words that tell of something that will happen before it ever happens. Four to five hundred years before Jesus was born, God led men to tell us facts about Jesus. These facts are prophecies.

RESURRECTION

To come back from the dead. Jesus died on the cross but three days later he came back to life. We say Jesus was resurrected when he came back to life.

SAVIOR

A person who rescues someone or something else. Jesus can rescue us from our sin. Jesus wants to be our Savior.

SIN

Choosing our own selfish way to live, and not choosing to live by God's rules.

SINS

The things we choose to say, do, or think which the Bible tells us are wrong and are against God's will, such as lying, cheating, and stealing.

THE WORLD

When we say "the world's Big Lie," we are using the word world to mean most of the people around us. In Lesson One we learn that most people (the world) do not think they need a friendship with God.

Group Leader's
EVALUATION FORM

1. How many children participated in this course? _____

2. Did you use:
    ❏ The Older Children's Workbooks
    ❏ The Younger Children's Workbooks
    ❏ Both

3. Did the church youth group use *The Revolt* Workbook or *The Revolt* Video Course?
    ❏ Yes   ❏ No

4. Did the church adult group use the *Belief Matters* Workbook or *Belief Matters* Video Course?
    ❏ Yes   ❏ No

5. On a scale of 1 to 10 (10 being the highest) how would you rate:

    a) The usefulness of the *True or False* Leaders Guide _____

    b) The responsiveness and interaction of your children _____

6. How effective would you say this course was in clarifying and deepening your children's conviction and commitment to Christ?
    ❏ Extremely ❏ Somewhat ❏ Little

7. Please give any comment you feel would be helpful to us.

    _____
    _____
    _____
    _____
    _____

Please mail to:
    Dave Bellis
    P.O. Box 4126
    Copley, OH 44321

True or False
Leaders Notes

True or False
Leaders Notes

Leaders Notes

True or False

Leaders Notes

True or False

Leaders Notes

True or False
Leaders Notes

True or False
Leaders Notes